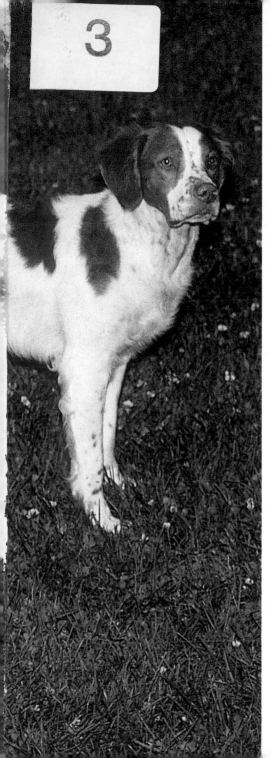

Dan Rice, DVM

Brittanys

Everything about Purchase, Care,
Nutrition, Behavior, and Training

With 49 Color Photographs

Illustrations by Tana Hakanson

BARRON'S

About the Author

Dan Rice is a retired veterinarian from Colorado, presently pursuing a life-long avocation in writing. This is his seventh book for Barron's. Now living in Arizona with his wife Marilyn, Dan doesn't hunt anymore, but remembers the excitement and satisfaction of shooting over fine gundogs. The Brittany has long been a favorite of his, and writing this book was a labor of love.

Photo Credits

Barbara Augello: front cover, page 84; Paulette Braun: pages 4, 41, 53; Callea Photo: pages 25, 92 bottom; Kent and Donna Dannen: inside front cover, inside back cover, pages 45 top, 88 bottom, 93, 96, 100, 101 top; J. B. and H. N. Engel: pages 8, 17 bottom, 29, 37, 40, 48, 68, 72 top and bottom, 76, 81; Bonnie Nance: pages 44, 57, 56 left; Paola Visintini: pages 24, 32, 45 bottom, 69; Fran and David Phillips: pages 17 top, 21; Gene and Neveta Salmon: pages 33, 64; Ralph and Mary Sleeper: pages 9, 12 right, Judith Strom: back cover, pages 13, 16 top and bottom, 20, 28, 49, 56 right, 61, 65 top and bottom, 73, 89, 97; Chuck and Sandy Tatham: page 92 top; Kenneth Thomas: page 101 bottom; Mary Walker: page 121.

All inquiries should be addressed to:
Barron's Educational Series, Inc.
250 Wireless Boulevard
Hauppauge, NY 11788
http://www.barronseduc.com

International Standard Book No. 0-7641-0448-9
Library of Congress Catalog Card No. 98-13204

Library of Congress Cataloging-in-Publication Data

Rice, Dan, 1933-
    Brittanys : everything about purchase, care, nutrition, behavior, and training / Dan Rice ; illustrations by Tana Hakanson.
        p.   cm.—(A complete pet owner's manual)
    Includes bibliographical references (p. 99) and index.
    ISBN 0–7641-0448-9
    1. Brittany. I. Title. II. Series.
SF429.B78R5   1998
636.752—dc21
98-13204

Printed in Hong Kong

98765432

Dedication and Acknowledgments

This book is dedicated to Brittany breeders and owners everywhere. Never before have I met with such enthusiasm from a group of dog fanciers. It is only with the superb cooperation of many Brittany authorities that this book has been written. A special thanks is due to Drs. Hal and Jodi Engel who evaluated the manuscript, made many suggestions, and furnished lots of pictures, and to Eugene and Bettye Wells who furnished some of the anecdotes. Dr. Gail Schmieder and Anthony and Nancy Morabito lent their experience and comments, and Fran Phillips came through with an abundance of pictures and information about the breed. Gene and Neveta Salmon shared their 30 years of Brittany ownership; Vernon and Brenda Jordan, Frank and Donna Pride contributed as well. The limited size and scope of this Pet Owner's Manual couldn't do justice to the wealth of information that I have accumulated about the Brittany, and I hope I haven't disappointed any of these wonderful Brittany fanciers.

A special thanks goes out to Barron's Managing Editor, Grace Freedson, and Project Editor, Mary Falcon. Without them this book would be just a dream.

Important Note

This pet owner's guide tells the reader how to buy and care for a Brittany dog. The author and the publisher consider it important to point out that the advice given in the book is meant primarily for normally developed puppies from a good breeder—that is, dogs of excellent physical health and good character.

Anyone who adopts a fully grown dog should be aware that the animal has already formed its basic impressions of human beings. The new owner should watch the animal carefully, including its behavior toward humans, and should meet the previous owner. If the dog comes from a shelter, it may be possible to get some information on the dog's background and peculiarities there. There are dogs that, as a result of bad experiences with humans, behave in an unnatural manner or may even bite. Only people that have experience with dogs should take in such animals.

Caution is further advised in the association of children with dogs, in meeting with other dogs, and in exercising the dog without a leash.

Even well-behaved and carefully supervised dogs sometimes do damage to someone else's property or cause accidents. It is therefore in the owner's interest to be adequately insured against such eventualities, and we strongly urge all dog owners to purchase a liability policy that covers their dog.

Contents

Am I a happy pup? You bet!

Introduction

Origin of *Canis Familiaris*

Until recently, the exact origin of *Canis familiaris,* the domestic dog, remained obscure in spite of the investigations of scores of learned researchers. Scientific analyses using mitochondrial (intracellular) DNA has now indicated that all dog breeds are descendants of the wolf. This discovery is hard to believe when we consider the many types, shapes, sizes, and colors of domestic dogs. To be sure there are also various sizes and colors of wolves. Those of the Northern Hemisphere are larger than those of the southern climates, and smaller races also are indigenous to India and China.

Nevertheless, wolves and dogs share many common characteristics. Both are classified as carnivores by their teeth, which are adapted to seizing, slicing, and tearing. Both have well-developed and extremely acute olfactory (smelling) and auditory (hearing) senses. A pack of domestic dogs, like their progenitors, follow the guidance of the dominant pack leader (alpha dog). Wild dogs and wolves maintain central headquarters, regions, or dens, that they defend, and they routinely deposit scent trails to stake out the boundaries of those areas.

If one concedes that dogs descended from wolves, there is still one question that will remain: Does my Brittany and your Mexican Hairless share common ancestry with Uncle Henry's Mastiff and Grandma's Pug? If so, how can it be?

Human Influence

This much is certain: In the centuries since domestication, the dog has earned its title as "best friend."

Humans and canines have established a symbiotic relationship that predates written history. This mutually beneficial association is depicted in petroglyphs that decorate the living room walls of cave dweller's homes. Likewise, the paintings and sculptures of dogs found among relics and artifacts of ancient civilizations further confirm this association between humans and canines.

Domestication

How did the wild canine and humans first form their partnerships? The answer to this provocative question is buried in antiquity. It is logical to assume that "dogs" first existed apart from human society. They were probably wild carnivores that survived by hunting, killing, and eating their prey. The present-day wild cousins of *Canis familiaris* give us visible evidence of their ancestor's probable habits and lifestyles.

Being intelligent creatures, dogs very likely joined human company, seeking an easily available source of food and shelter. Dogs may have followed prehistoric human leaders in hunts, ingesting the scraps from a kill, and later assisting those humans in obtaining and protecting their food. At some point, humans may have substituted themselves for alpha dogs and assumed leadership and dominance in the packs. Dogs that refused to submit to human domination were eliminated; they were rejected from the human's society or they provided meat for the stew pots and pelts for clothing. By this primitive, unplanned selective breeding, the surviving dogs became helpmates to the people who kept them.

Dogs' hunting expertise, guarding ability, and their acceptance of subservient roles in society were soon recognized. Their presence made human existence much easier and perhaps safer. Furry canines were used to provide warmth; they were trained as guard dogs, hunting assistants, and companions, and later as herders; they soon earned the title "man's best friend."

Throughout history, dogs have served people in many roles. It is only natural that the dominant human should select and breed dogs of the size, strength, coat, and temperament that please them or fill their particular needs. Thus we now have hundreds of different dog breeds from which to choose, and it is a wonder of nature that all trace their origin to wolves.

Dog's Uses

Great Danes were originally bred to their magnificent size and strength to hunt bears, boars, and other big game. Siberian Huskies and Alaskan Malamutes developed protective coats to withstand bitter winters, and were selected for their stamina to pull loaded sleds in the deep snow. Rangy, sleek gazehounds such as the Irish wolfhound, Saluki, and Greyhound were selectively bred for the speed and endurance to course wolves, elk, hares, or other game. Coonhounds and Bloodhounds were chosen for their great scenting powers and stamina to follow a trail for miles. Gigantic mastiffs were selectively bred to guard and defend property, while the diminutive Mexican Hairless was developed as a lap dog. The Saint Bernard was bred for high mountain rescue in a hospice in the Alps, and the Lhasa Apso was a cherished Tibetan temple dog. In some primitive societies, dogs are still raised for their meat and pelts.

Sporting breeds like the Brittany were originally bred for their specialized abilities to find and retrieve upland game birds.

Selective Breeding

New genetic engineering techniques such as gene splicing and chromosome manipulations may produce dynamic changes in a single generation of animals. Those high-tech laboratory processes aren't necessary, however, to produce new dog breeds or varieties within a breed. Dogs are equipped with an easily manipulated genetic structure, one that allows conformation changes to be altered quickly by selective breeding.

Dogs can raise at least one litter every year and are capable of reproducing before one year of age. It is therefore quite possible for a new generation to be spawned annually. (Although that level of reproduction may be possible, it is irresponsible for conscientious dog breeders to consider such a practice today.)

Dogs of the same genotype (genetic properties) have the capacity to vary in phenotype (visible and behavioral properties). Phenotypic changes are produced in nature by the interaction of genotype with the environment. By choosing dogs that display certain traits, and by using those dogs in a breeding program, many canine physical characteristics can be molded and changed rather easily. This process is known as selective breeding.

You might wish to develop a darker coat on your Brittanys. By careful selection of a few dogs that possess the darker coats, a gene pool is quickly established that possesses the "dark coat" phenotype. In each generation of puppies produced from those specially chosen parents, only the offspring with the darkest coats are mated. Within a few generations, dark coats should be routinely seen in a majority of puppies produced. The selected dark coat characteristic is quickly stamped on the progeny of that bloodline.

This simplified, hypothetical example is intended only to illustrate the concept of canine phenotypic malleability, or the plasticity of canine characteristics. There are many pitfalls to dog breeding that is based on selection for a single physical characteristic, and the example provided is not meant to advocate such activity.

Careful selective breeding may or may not be the answer to the origin of the hundreds of breeds and the multitude of sizes, shapes, temperaments, and uses of dogs that presently populate the earth. It is certainly the method used to produce minor phenotypic changes such as behavior modification, various coat types, and color patterns that are seen in the Brittany breed.

Rejected pets are abandoned in great numbers in the United States.

Human Stewardship

The availability of a great variety of dogs isn't all good news. A well-trained Brittany is seen and admired, its beautiful personality and superb intelligence are duly appreciated. A naive person might assume that all Brittanys somehow automatically grow up with those credentials. Further demonstrating that artless assumption, a Brittany puppy is purchased without investigating the patience, time, and work required to train it. A year later, the dog has become a nuisance, a liability that results from no fault of its own.

Lack of planning has led to the destruction of millions of wonderful canine pets that were obtained without thought by well-meaning families. Unfortunately, every breed is occasionally caught up in this scenario and winds up in the dog warden's truck or in a kennel operated by a Brittany rescue organization.

Rejected, unwanted American pets now number in the hundreds of thousands in the United States. They occupy dog pounds, breed rescue services, and animal shelters across the country. When those facilities can no longer house them, they are euthanized (put to sleep) in enormous numbers.

Only responsible dog owners and breeders can control canine overpopulation. That includes all of us who obtain dogs and don't have them sexually neutered before they reach reproductive age. Nearly as irresponsible are those of us who adopt a dog and fail to train it, teach it manners, and give it something to do. We must accept the role of stewards of our pets when we obtain a dog. That is critically important whether shopping for a purebred, trainable Brittany or a mixed-breed pup for a child's pet.

Breeders should employ a neutering policy for all pets sold; written contracts can be used to ensure that the policy is followed. All prospective dog breeders should be aware that only the best examples of their chosen breed should be used in a breeding program. Irresponsible owners who assume that all registered dogs are

Brittanys have become popular because of their temperament.

Until recently, the official breed name was "Brittany Spaniel." "Spaniel" literally means "Spanish dog." Whether or not Spain had some hand in developing the Brittany is problematical. Spaniels, pointers, and setters may have all originated in Spain, and the name "spaniel" could be a corruption of "Hispana," or "Espanol."

Regardless of the source of its name, the modern Brittany has the historical scenting ability of the famous bird dogs of Europe. Its colors and general type are similar to the other setters, pointers, and spaniels of coastal France, Holland, England, Flanders, and Germany. Many of the bird-hunting dogs of Great Britain and Wales, notably the Welsh Springer Spaniel and some of the setters, are similar in appearance to the Brittany, and may share ancestry with it.

Pointers and setters are usually faster, leggier, lighter, and have a wider hunting range than spaniels. As their name implies, they point their quarry and attempt to keep it pinned down until the hunter is within shooting distance. In those regards, the Brittany belongs to the pointer-setter types of hunting dogs.

The Brittany shares characteristics other than color and type with these hunting dogs. It is a scenting dog, an instinctive pointer with the ability to "set" or hold its quarry in cover.

"Setting" game birds predates easily accessible gunpowder and the sport of shooting. Ancient "setters" would scent a covey of birds, point them, and pin them down. The hunters would then throw large nets over the cover occupied by the birds, and the birds were thus captured alive. This technique has been used in recent history to capture wild game birds that are used in organized shoots.

Setters were also used quite efficiently in hunting game birds with falcons. After the bird dogs pointed and

"breeding quality" exacerbate the dog overpopulation problem.

If you find yourself with a Brittany that you can't keep, contact the Brittany club in your area or the American Brittany Club. There is also a Brittany rescue association that will help you deal with your problem. Addresses are provided in the back of this book.

A Rose by Any Other Name

The Brittany province of France seems to be the source of the Brittany name; however, other evidence connects the name "Brittany" to Bretagne, or Britannia, which is part of England, rather than France. The paradox that surrounds the Brittany's name is no less confusing than the actual origin of the breed.

Brittany is an isolated province of northwest France that was heavily influenced by a Celtic background, distinguishing it from other regions of the country. The province got its name from British Celts who moved to the region subsequent to the withdrawal of Rome. Brittany has been under both French and British domination at various times in history.

set a covey of birds, the hunting falcons of the landed gentry were made ready, then the game birds were flushed and the falcons attacked them in the air.

Brittany History

The Brittany is one of Europe's oldest hunting breeds, but its specific ancestry is subject to debate. Since no written history is available prior to the mid-1800s, we must refer to paintings of the seventeenth century for descriptions and locations of earlier dogs.

Various references join the Brittany's ancestors with the Irish invaders of France. Those people were avid wildfowlers and brought with them the long-tailed Irish Red and White Setter. That breed dates from the eighteenth century and is believed to be the progenitor of the Irish Setter as well. Some writers refer to the English sportsmen who went to Brittany, France to shoot woodcock; they often took along their English Setters that might have been crossed with a Breton or a dog that was native to Brittany. There is no question that the early Brittanys were sporting dogs, whether or not they shared origin with the Irish Setter centuries ago.

An English sportsman is said to have developed the earliest tailless Brittanys in France in about 1850 as woodcock hunting dogs. An imported, naturally bob-tailed, lemon-and-white dog was bred to a mahogany-and-white native hunting bitch to produce those dogs. The Brittany as we know it today probably dates from those crosses.

Arthur Enaud who lived in the valley of Douron, France is principally responsible for the popular orange and white colored Brittany. To fix these colors, to combat the degeneration of inbreeding, and to increase the dogs' scenting abilities, Enaud is thought to have crossed the Italian Bracco and the Braque de Bourbonnais with his Brittanys. Braques were developed as pointing breeds in France. The tailless

Brittanys are typical pointers and have little in common with "spaniels."

characteristic of the Brittany was also more firmly fixed by the Braque de Bourbonnais, which possessed a naturally bobbed tail. The early French standards required that all Brittany puppies were to be born tailless, but that requirement was soon abandoned. Those outcrosses are thought to be the last such mixing of breeds that occurred in the foundation of the Brittany. This also explains why a few of the Brittanys of today are born tailless.

The Brittany in America

Oddly, the early American popularity of the Brittany was due in part to the influence of a Frenchman who lived in Vera Cruz, Mexico. J. Pugibet imported Brittanys from France to hunt in Yucatan, Mexico. A friend of Pugibet, Louis Thebaud, lived in New Jersey, but often hunted in Mexico. Thebaud was so impressed with the dogs that he imported them into the United States. He established a Brittany breeding program with Eudore Chevier, a French Canadian who lived in Winnipeg, Manitoba. Thebaud helped form the Brittany

The Brittany is an old European breed.

Spaniel Club of North America, which merged with the American Brittany Club in 1942.

The Brittany has been recognized in the United States since the 1930s. From 1934 until 1982, the American Kennel Club (AKC) registered Brittanys as "Spaniel, Brittany." The Brittany was known as the "world's only pointing spaniel" and was possibly classified as a spaniel because it characteristically worked within range of the hunter's gun and because it would flush game birds in that range.

When the AKC recognized the first Brittany club, a petition was circulated to change the breed name to "Brittany." The request was denied by the AKC based on the registration name in other countries, including the country of origin (whatever country that might have been).

The Brittany successfully threw off its spaniel classification in the United States, and the breed name was officially changed to "Brittany" on September 1, 1982. The AKC, in response to the national breed club's request, dropped "Spaniel" in spite of the nomenclature inconsistency with other countries. Elsewhere in the world, the Brittany of today continues to be called the "Brittany Spaniel."

This name change seems well justified for several reasons. The Brittany's conformation differs significantly from most spaniels in that the Brittany has a much lighter build. Its ears are shorter and set higher, and in general the dog is leggier than most spaniels. Its coat is not the heavy type that is characteristic of cockers or springers. The spaniel is basically a flushing dog, whereas the Brittany is a pointer.

Brittany field trial competition in the United States has always been held with the pointers and setters and not with spaniels or other water-retrieving dogs. Therefore, the Brittany is similar to setters and pointers in looks and function, and the new name seems to fit the Brittany in every respect. Why the short-eared, square-bodied, leggy Brittany was designated as a spaniel is still open to conjecture.

Early Show History

Brittanys were first shown at the Paris dog show of 1900, and official French recognition of the breed came in 1905 when an orange-and-white male was registered in France under the official breed name "l'epagneul Breton," or its English equivalent, "Brittany Spaniel."

French dog shows thereafter had entries of at least 75 Brittanys. As a show dog, the Brittany improved in type and uniformity in the early 1900s. By 1925 more than 100 Brittanys were entered in a show at Rennes, France. The dog shows of that era and beyond were instrumental in preserving many breeds that would have otherwise become extinct. Breeds and strains were saved by fanciers and were exhibited in dog shows. The depressed economy of that period of European history dictated that only the best of these dogs was kept as breeding stock.

Appreciating Your Brittany

Dual-Purpose Dog

It has been said of Brittanys that they have passed the test on every type of game for which pointing dogs are used. They have the disposition of the best house pet and companion, yet retain a passion for hunting. The American Brittany Club and Brittany breeders of the United States have committed themselves to preserve the Brittany as a dual-purpose dog, which means that there is little or no differences within the breed between field trial dogs and conformation show dogs.

Many sporting breeds have started out with similar intentions, but over the years, have shown a definite split in purposes. A true dual-purpose dog can leave the field one day, have a bath, and win in a conformation show the next day.

This dual-role determination by Brittany fanciers has made it necessary for Brittany clubs to instruct show judges in what the Brittany's appearance must be. It means that concerned Brittany breeders must support and compete in both phases of the fancy. The result is that field Brittanys maintain the same coat, movement, temperament, and size as conformation show dogs.

One Brittany owner has been working with the breed for 25 years, has raised six litters, and has been a judge and a professional handler for more than 12 years. She describes the Brittany as the "ideal" dog. She has "finished" or earned the AKC Champion of Record Title on about 30 Brittanys and has seven dual champions to her credit. This Brittany enthusiast, like many other breeders, trainers, and handlers has found that the well-bred Brittany is equally at home in the show ring or field.

By the standards of breeds such as the English Setter and Cocker Spaniel, with their long, silky coats, the Brittany isn't a "pretty" dog. It is difficult to judge the vibrant color and airy flowing grace of an Irish Setter against the quick, productive movement of a Brittany. It's probably for those reasons that the Brittany hasn't won its fair share of "Best In Group" or "Best In Show" awards in all-breed shows.

This oversight is more than compensated by the fact that the Brittany has produced more dual champions than any other breed. Brittany fanciers have always recognized the beauty of intelligence, soundness, balance, and symmetry of motion. These fanciers continue to value and cultivate these features in their hunting and competition dogs.

The Versatile Brittany

After its introduction into the United States, the Brittany grew slowly in popularity and acceptance. The AKC registered 11,539 Brittanys in 1996, making them thirty-fourth in popularity. This rank is down 1 percent from 1995 when they were thirty-second in popularity with 11,618 dogs registered. They held the twenty-eighth place in AKC registrations in 1992 with 14,901. Only four bird dog breeds rank ahead of the Brittany in popularity.

Gun Dog

The breed is an outstanding performance dog, with a fantastic nose and superb hunting style. With these attributes it's no wonder that the breed is one of the most esteemed hunting dogs in the United States today. The Brittany is a medium-sized dog with an acute sense of smell and an excellent retrieving ability. Because its natural pointing instinct is easily developed, the Brittany is a fine choice as an upland bird-hunting dog.

The Brittany is known as a superb woodcock dog that is also successful in locating grouse. The Brittany will enter ponds and streams to retrieve waterfowl, and like the spaniels, pointers, and setters, it uses windborne scents to locate its quarry.

In the field, the Brittany works well in any terrain and in most climates. In the past, before the name change, it was described as "a spaniel with a difference," because it points its birds, instead of immediately flushing them. It endures the cold very well and can be trained to hunt hare as well as partridge and other upland birds. It is a strong, lively, energetic hunter that rarely lacks endurance, as this story illustrates.

"Star" and her handler were cleaning up a field in the Arizona shooting preserve. She had pointed, set, and retrieved several pheasants during a fine afternoon's shooting when she pointed another bird. The pheasant was flushed, and the handler shot the bird, but its rapid flight caused it to sail across the strong-running river. As it fell into the brush on the far side of the river, Star hit the water like a Chesapeake, swam across, nosed out the bird, and retrieved it. A nice bit of swimming for an upland bird dog!

The Brittany's primary popularity in the United States has come from hunting and field trial enthusiasts and weekend bird shooters. This is a bird

The versatile Brittany is at home in the field or yard.

Brittanys are excellent family dogs.

Some Brittanys begin to retrieve at a very young age.

dog that usually quarters closely in the field, making it quite adaptable to the limited shooting areas of today. It is easily trained and is a natural retriever. It is truly a dog for all hunters. It has been called the apartment-dweller's weekend gun dog and may well serve such a purpose. An example might help illustrate how a natural hunter like the Brittany responds to an unusual situation.

"Jessie" was in Arizona to hunt chukar. She pointed a bird, which was flushed, and the hunters fired. The bird continued to fly but dropped a leg. The field being hunted was on a river-bank, and thick brush covered both sides of the water. Jessie was sent across the river for the bird, and she soon disappeared into the dense cover on the far side. She was gone for a long while, and after a time the hunters began to worry. They called and blew the whistle, but she didn't respond. Finally, she appeared on the far bank, swam across the river, and proudly presented the chukar to the hunters. It was still alive!

Although some Brittanys are hunted as early as six months of age, they probably reach their prime between four and five years. They are clever, biddable dogs that show very little stubbornness in the field.

Family Dog

For those who are not interested in hunting, but do appreciate the active qualities and temperaments of hunting dogs, the beautiful Brittany easily adapts to a life of dog shows or playing with the kids. Its size makes it acceptable as an urban backyard pet. It is a great companion for the jogger or runner and is capable of carrying a pack with the owner's water supply. It is a healthy, happy dog that is playful and trustworthy and loves children.

The Brittany is a superb family dog, loyal and faithful whether used in the field or confined to the backyard. It is unique among sporting dogs; its coat is relatively short, dense, flat, or wavy, never excessively feathered, and doesn't require a great deal of trimming.

Because the Brittany is sensitive and must be handled gently, it is sometimes described as a timid dog. In general that isn't true; it is typically gentle, happy, and fun loving. Timidity or shyness is not characteristic of the breed, although unthinking adults and children can cause those traits to develop. It is a bright, intelligent dog that is anxious to please its owners, as this quote from a breeder with 25 years experience indicates. "A Brittany would die for you! These dogs love life and people and want to do anything to please you. They are sensitive and highly manipulative, and sometimes are smarter than their owners, so they are best placed with intelligent, friendly, and active families."

The friendly Brittany doesn't respond well to rough treatment; corrective-training measures must be meted out with caution. That doesn't mean that it can't tolerate correction. It is a strong, tough dog with a gentle disposition and a great heart, and its best home is with active, mild-tempered, patient owners.

Brittany breeders describe their dogs as friendly and nonaggressive; easy dogs to housebreak that make great pets for kids. They are characteristically inquisitive, very intelligent, and get along well with other pets.

The Brittany is a dual-purpose dog that, according to most breeders, will excel in showing or fieldwork, or both, depending on the owner's skill and interest. The general belief is that if Brittanys are bred to meet the standard, they will do well in either endeavor. More than one owner takes her Brittany from field competition on one day, brushes him out and enters him in a conformation show the next day.

Think Before You Buy

Before buying a Brittany, remember that this breed isn't the ideal dog for every family, regardless of its exceptional qualities. You should never purchase any dog on a whim, least of all a Brittany. Its heritage is that of a sporting field dog, meaning that it shouldn't be compared to small house pets that require minimal exercise or attention. Because it is an active dog, time and space must be provided for it to expend that energy. Unless you lead an active, outdoor life and plan to spend a great deal of time with your new Brittany, maybe you should rethink your selection.

Selecting Your Brittany

Are You Ready for a Dog?

Before deciding on a specific breed, you should ask yourself a few questions regarding a new dog in the family. Impulse buying often leads to disappointment, and it is usually disastrous when purchasing a pet. This dog will share your home and heart for many years, and the decision to obtain it should be discussed with all household members. A simplified checklist follows that contains many items you should consider before purchasing a new dog. The majority of these questions should be answered in the affirmative before you begin to search for your Brittany.

• Is there a place in your life for an animal that requires love and attention? Do you have time to spend with a new pet? Unfortunately, this item is frequently overlooked, especially if there are young children in the family. Grownups often make the mistake of delegating a puppy's care to a four- or five-year-old child who is too young to take responsibility for its care. This is a serious error in judgment. A puppy isn't likely to mature into a well-mannered dog, a pet that you will be proud to have in your home, unless it receives many hours of your attention.

• Are you prepared to furnish the new puppy with adequate housing? In most cases, that means a fenced yard and a warm, dry doghouse. If the Brittany pup is going to share your home, do you have an area to dedicate to its use during the period of housebreaking?

• Have you calculated the ongoing cost of dog ownership? The original price of a dog is only the tip of the iceberg. There are initial and annual vaccinations to pay for and neutering or spaying fees to consider. Your Brittany will deserve the best food; tick, flea, and heartworm control must be provided. Consider the cost of dishes, beds, collars, and leashes.

• If you plan to use your Brittany for bird hunting or field trials, have you calculated the training costs? Maintaining a competition hunting dog is a separate subject with an additional price tag.

• Have you found someone who will care for your dog when you are away from home? Have you investigated boarding kennels or do you have reliable friends who will care for your Brittany when you aren't able to do so?

Timing

Planning is important. In order to start a puppy out correctly, everyone in the family must be ready for him. Don't buy your puppy immediately before the holidays. Confusion reigns in most households around Christmas time, and the pup's needs may be lost in the rush. There are many events that take a great deal of your time during that busy period. A preferred plan is to purchase dog equipment to place under the Christmas tree. Bring the pup home later, after the celebration is over, the tree is gone, and the family has settled into their normal routine. Then you and your family will have time to focus on the new Brittany.

When do you usually take a vacation? If you plan to be gone the first few weeks of July, don't bring a new pup home in May or June. Wait until

A lonely puppy is an unhappy puppy.

after the household is quiet and the usual routine is established before you begin housebreaking and leash training. It is a serious mistake to start those efforts and then pass them off to someone else.

Puppies require more than just a place to live.

If your home is going to be filled with friends or relatives during spring break, look for a pup after that time has passed. Extra people to play with the pup might seem like a good idea, but they are counterproductive if they upset your training program.

Is the Brittany the Right Dog?

There were 3,319 Brittany litters registered by the AKC in 1996 and that number has remained relatively constant for the last several years. This figure indicates a continued interest in the breed in the United States, but not an oversupply of puppies. When breeds become No. 1 in popularity, they often attract too much attention and are overbred. The Brittany hasn't risen to that popularity height yet and hopefully it never will. Responsible breeders still maintain good control over this breed.

Health and Life Expectancy

Brittanys, being generally healthy dogs, are among the smaller hunting breeds and are usually destined to live long lives. It is common for Brittanys to live 12 years; some even reach the age of 14 or 15. The secret to good health and longevity for our dogs isn't much different from our own. A preventive medicine program that is followed throughout life is of utmost importance.

Proper nutrition and exercise are equally important to your pet's longevity, as is the protection of confinement to a yard or kennel. Likewise, grooming and coat care are fundamental to a dog's general health. Brittanys are inquisitive, intelligent pets, and special attention should be given to keeping them as busy as possible. If you hunt, exercise may not be a problem, but if your hunting is only done for a few hours on an occasional October weekend, that may not supply enough exercise for a Brittany.

Companion or conformation show dogs must receive regular playtimes or else they will become melancholic or bored and will develop nuisance habits such as chewing or digging. Walks with the dog and regular playtimes can't be overdone.

Veterinary Opinion

In choosing the right dog for your family, consult with knowledgeable people. Talk with a veterinarian about your choice of breed. In all probability, he or she has had experience with Brittanys and will be able to provide insights into your selection. Picking the right family pet involves long-range planning, and you can use all the help you can get. A veterinarian's opinion is invaluable; she or he handles dogs by the dozens every day and has firsthand experience with the idiosyncrasies of many breeds.

A prepurchase discussion with your veterinarian serves many purposes. If you ask, you will receive a general idea of the expense involved in routine dog care. You can also receive ideas about housing and boarding kennels in your area. Risks of certain diseases that are indigenous to your region of the country can be discussed. Hereditary conditions that are seen in the Brittany can be outlined, and you may receive advice on how to detect commonly recognized problems. A veterinarian may recommend Brittany breeders, owners, and trainers in your locality.

Choosing the Right Brittany

Male or Female

The sex of your pet is mainly a matter of personal preference. Some of us like the temperament of females; others prefer masculine characteristics. There is very little difference in the sexes when seeking a pet that is to be neutered at or before adulthood.

Dams often stop feeding their litter by six weeks.

Male dogs generally tend to be more aggressive than females, but this does not seem to be a characteristic of Brittanys. Females are usually more gentle than males, but this too is relative. Remember the heritage of the Brittany. Hunting is the Brittany's life; the breed was developed as a hunting dog, and

This companion puppy seems quite content.

eagerness to work and play will dominate both sexes. Both sexes are loyal, trainable, affectionate, and playful.

If a female is chosen, the cost of spaying might be a bit higher than the cost of neutering a male; but when prorated over the life of the dog, that is a minor consideration. Both sexes may be trained with the same degree of success. The Brittany—whether male or female—is quick to learn, eager to please, and requires a minimum of correction.

There is no appreciable difference in the health care of dogs of either sex, provided that they are spayed or neutered. If you are considering showing your Brittany, it can't be neutered, and you must remember that females come in heat approximately every six months. You can enjoy hunting, obedience, agility, and 4-H competition with a neutered Brittany.

Appropriate Age of Puppy

Puppies' mothers often stop feeding their puppies by six weeks of age. Prior to that time, and for the next couple of weeks, the pups learn to socialize with their dam and members of their litter. It is a serious mistake to remove them from their dam and siblings before that time. From birth to eight weeks, while associating with their littermates, they learn valuable lessons about getting along with other dogs. One breeder has suggested that young Brittany puppies be introduced to male dogs as well. The sire of a litter "turns to mush" when faced with squirming puppies and often takes his turn in licking and nurturing the litter.

Most breeders will keep puppies until they are at least seven to ten weeks old. You should try to bring the pup into your home as early as possible following that period. The socialization period of puppies with humans extends from about three weeks to three months of age. It is during this important bonding time that the pup should be introduced to your family. This is the period when the puppy will best learn vital lessons that stay with him the rest of his life. Puppies will accept leash training when six to eight weeks old. The time before 12 weeks is also the period that bad habits may be easily learned; be always mindful of this, because these habits are deeply imprinted in a puppy's mind as well.

If that time passes by, and you aren't able to bring the pup home before it is three months old, choose a puppy that has been handled as much as possible. Pups that mature without human companionship and are kept exclusively with other dogs during their human bonding period may not bond to their owners and may prove to be poor companions. Brittanys are, however, very human-oriented dogs and with love and attention, they will usually bond with an attentive and caring family well into adulthood. They are among the breeds that are most easily adopted as adults from shelters.

The best pet is one that has been left with the litter, but has been regularly handled by the breeder's family from shortly after birth until eight weeks of age. When the puppy goes to its permanent home at eight weeks of age, it will bond to its new family quickly.

Temperament

Don't overlook temperament when choosing a puppy. Although it is often difficult to pick out temperament differences in a litter of frisky puppies, the parents will often give you a clue as to what their offspring's attitude will be like when they grow up. Shy dogs don't usually make good hunters, or at least they will be more difficult to train and handle. Viciousness isn't a typical trait of the Brittany, but stay away from puppies whose sire or dam is difficult to handle.

Type of Brittany

Gun Dogs

When choosing a shooting dog, similar guidelines should be employed as when choosing a companion or show dog, but with a few added requirements. Shooting dogs are usually exposed to guns and gunfire at a fairly early age and certainly before they are sold as hunting prospects. They should have a keen inherent interest in retrieving. At 6 to 12 weeks of age they should pick up and carry a ball, dummy, sock, or a bird wing.

Potential gun dog puppies can't be critically evaluated based on their retrieving interest or ability. Most Brittanys will perform those functions whether or not they are the progeny of proven shooting dogs. Probably the most reliable measure of a hunting Brittany at the age of eight or ten weeks is the performance of its parents and grandparents.

Field Trial Dogs

If you wish to locate a Brittany to compete in formal field trials, the best advice is to seek better advice than you can find in any book. Talk to individuals who are involved with field trials. Take their advice regarding kennels that have routinely raised winning dogs. Seek out the advice of a successful professional trainer. Attend field trials and meet the people who participate. Watch the field Brittanys perform; talk to their owners. The American Kennel Club (AKC) or American Brittany Club (ABC) can refer you to competition field trials in your region.

Show Dogs

Conformation show dogs will probably be available from the same kennels that produce field trial dogs. You will have a better than average chance of acquiring a show dog from a breeder that has ribbons and rosettes from AKC shows hanging on the walls and the dogs that won those awards living in their kennel.

Out of every litter of Brittanys from "show" parents perhaps only one or two puppies are destined to have an excellent career as show dogs. The breeder often keeps those puppies until three or four months of age to watch their development. Remember there really shouldn't be any notable difference between show-quality puppies and gun dogs. Kennels that raise field dogs should be able to supply your need for a show dog and vice versa.

Companion Dogs

While it seems a shame to consign a wonderful hunting dog to a backyard where it never has the opportunity to point or retrieve game, the Brittany doesn't seem to mind. This dog has been bred for generations to hunt, but like most other hunting breeds, its personality is malleable, and it will adapt to the lifestyle of a family pet quite well and without problems.

Any Brittany breeder may supply pets. Every litter includes some pups that don't quite meet the requirements of competition show or hunting dogs. A puppy's pedigree may be stippled with Champions that indicate careful breeding, but perhaps he has some minor color or conformational fault that isn't conducive to a successful performance career. Such a pup is usually sold for less than the choice puppies, but he will have all of the important characteristics of those pups.

Finding the Right Breeder

Breeders may be located in any number of ways. The ABC is a fine place to start. Write to them at the address found in the back of this book. Ask for a list of ABC members in your locality. Contact the ABC Regional club secretary. That name may be obtained from the ABC or from the

Liver and white Brittanys occur in many purebred litters.

AKC, and he or she will be able to furnish names of Brittany breeders and trainers in your area. The AKC Internet site (http://AKC.org) provides links to pages of information about Brittanys.

To meet Brittany fanciers, go to a dog show in your part of the country. Attend field trials, hunting tests, and agility trials where you will make contacts that are invaluable if you are looking for a performance dog. Various dog magazines usually carry advertisements for Brittanys. Information about shows and trials may be obtained from the *American Kennel Club Gazette*, a monthly publication of the AKC. It also contains a breed listing with many kennel advertisements. *The American Brittany* is a monthly magazine that is published by the ABC, and it is an excellent source of contacts.

Look for Brittany ads in your local newspaper—but beware! Legitimate breeders do advertise in newspapers, but a newspaper ad may represent backyard breeders who aren't interested in the betterment of the breed. They also may promote puppies that originate in puppy mills. Puppy mills are establishments that own bitches of various breeds and produce hundreds of pups a year. They are notorious for producing poor quality pups of questionable health and parentage. It is easy to spot a puppy mill. When you arrive, a litter may be presented without the dam. If you ask to see her, an excuse is usually made, or if you see her, she is often in pitiful condition. If you gain entrance to the kennel, you will usually see various different breeds, crowded, dirty conditions, very little provision for exercise, and thin, overworked dams. These puppy mills should be avoided at all costs.

Pet shops may be a viable option for you. These shops usually don't have the dam or sire of a pup and rarely can you see the puppy's siblings. Many do, however, keep pedigrees and complete records of the puppies' origins, and you are thereby able to learn the name of the kennel in which the pup was raised and thus satisfy your requirements.

Neighborhood litters are a questionable source of companion dogs. Before you buy a backyard breeder's Brittany, be sure to examine the AKC registration and pedigree of the dam and sire. If the puppies aren't registered, beware! Backyard-bred puppies are often less expensive than kennel-raised dogs, and with good reason. They may prove to be fine pets, but it is unlikely that you will receive any guarantees of any kind.

Choosing a Healthy Puppy

When confronted with half a dozen happy, wriggling, tail-wagging little puppies, it is difficult to concentrate on health issues, but it is important that you do so before you choose a pup. Even a novice can inspect a pup and make a rough evaluation of its health, personality, and conformation to the Brittany standard before it is chosen to share your home.

Remember, a bad litter rarely yields good pups. If you see a collection of skinny, runny-eyed, lethargic, coughing puppies, don't handle them; run don't walk to the nearest exit. Don't make the mistake of taking a sick pup home for a trial, with the guarantee that it will get better in a day or two. Don't take the responsibility of buying a pup that is receiving medication. Raising a healthy, active puppy is challenge enough without buying more trouble. Everyone is entitled to begin his or her relationship with a healthy dog—don't settle for less!

Begin your home inspection by looking at both of the pup's parents if they are available. Your pup is a reflection of those adult dogs. If only the dam is owned, ask to see a picture of the sire, and if possible, pictures of his previous progeny. Don't rule the litter out because of the dam's physical condition; most

Everyone seems happy with this sleeping arrangement.

bitches look a bit rundown after weaning a litter of puppies. A good dam produces so much milk for the puppies that she is nutritionally drained after about six or eight weeks. She may be saggy, thinner than normal, and in poor coat when you see her. However, she should be clean and brushed, active and inquisitive. If available, look at her puppies from previous litters.

Look at the litter from a distance first.

The personality of the dam and sire is a vital part of puppy selection. If the adults are shy, timid, or reluctant to be handled, their puppies will probably have similar attitudes.

Performing an On-the-Spot Puppy Evaluation

Assuming that you are looking at pups that are about eight to ten weeks old, you won't catch every possible fault, but you will make a more intelligent choice if you follow these guidelines.

• Stand back and observe the litter from a few yards away. See if there are puppies that are reluctant to be picked up or petted. Make mental note of those that aren't joining in the tumbling and play. Perhaps one or two will run to hide behind their dam or nesting box. Those pups are often insecure and are probably a bit too young to leave their dam and siblings. Visit the litter more than once if the pups seem timid; a few days at this age makes a big difference.

• Watch for a puppy that is inquisitive and affectionate, but one that isn't aggressively attacking its siblings. Try to concentrate on puppies that don't hang back but are anxious to meet you. A certain amount of fear is normal when a stranger approaches a puppy, but you shouldn't choose a pup that is overtly shy.

• After you have narrowed the selection process to one or two puppies, squat or sit on the floor and carefully pick the puppy up. It is important to make yourself as small as possible when you first approach a pup. Lying on the floor (if practical) is an excellent posture. Don't grab a puppy as it runs by, and don't corner it somewhere. If the breeder's family has handled the pups, it will catch you; you won't have to chase it.

Reject a pup that immediately takes a defensive stance when you reach for it. If it snaps, screams, or otherwise seems frightened, it is probably not the pup for you.

Take the puppy into another room, away from the rest of the litter and watch its attitude when you set it on the floor. If one end is still wagging and the other is licking your hand, you are nearing a good selection.

• Cradle the puppy in your arms in an upside-down position and scratch its tummy and chin. It should let you do this with little objection and without squirming to right itself.

• After you have made friendly overtures to the puppy, stay settled on the floor and put the pup on your lap. Open its mouth and check its bite. The upper incisor teeth should overlap the lower front teeth, and they should touch. Any degree of gap between the upper and lower teeth (overshot or undershot) is a serious fault in the Brittany and should affect your choice, especially if you are looking for a dog to show or breed. A slight bite fault should not be a consideration if the puppy is purchased as a pet and will be neutered. It can still be entered in several competitions; its mouth defor-

Getting down to the pup's eye level often means getting your face washed.

mity won't interfere with eating, and it rarely causes any health problems.

• With the puppy standing or sitting, feel its abdomen for evidence of an umbilical hernia. A hernia may be identified as a protrusion of tissue about the size of a marble at the site of the navel. When the puppy is seven or eight weeks old, hernias are soft, and when they are pressed, they may disappear into the abdomen. Hernias are easily repaired, but they represent an additional expense to you.

• If selecting a male, check his scrotum for the presence of testicles. They should be descended into the scrotum by eight or ten weeks of age, and if not, they might never descend. That doesn't present a serious problem in a companion animal or a gun dog, but if you are considering entering your Brittany in competition, either leave the pup in the kennel until the testicles drop into place or pick another pup. (See the chapter on health care for more discussion.)

• Look at the puppy's eyes. The Brittany's eyes should not be "popped," or protruding. They should be clear, free of pus or matter, and the pup should not be squinting. At seven to eight weeks of age, the Brittany's eyes may still be blue. The puppy may be six to eight months old before the dark amber eyes appear. The color of the eyes isn't terribly important in pets. For show purposes, however, a dark amber color is preferred. The best indications of adult eye color are the parents. If both sire and dam have amber eyes, the pups will likely have that eye color when they are adults. As a rule of thumb, if the rim around the iris is dark, the dog's eyes will eventually become dark.

• The nose should also be visually examined. The Brittany has a brown, tan, or dark pink nose-rubber. It should be moist; dry nostrils with matter caked in the corners are sure signs of health problems.

If you can hold the squirming pup still for a moment, take the opportunity to check the bite.

• Finally, the puppy's tail is important in showing. It may be naturally bobbed or surgically shortened, but it should be short. A tail of more than four inches in length in an adult is severely penalized in dog shows. A totally tailless Brittany is preferable to one with too long a tail. All knowledgeable breeders will have the puppies tails docked and their dewclaws removed when the puppies are about three days old.

Health Records

You have found what you believe to be the perfect puppy, a bundle of energy that appears hale and healthy. There are several documents that should accompany your new Brittany. Among them are records of when and by whom the pup was vaccinated, the product used, and when another vaccination is needed.

Many documents accompany your Brittany pup.

The date on which a worm check was done and the results of that fecal exam should be included, along with the date of treatment for the parasites if the test was positive. The health papers should specify what product was used and the dose that was administered.

The records should include the date(s) of health examinations and the name and address of the veterinarian who performed the examination(s). If the pup was seen for an illness, that should be specified, as well as the name and dosage of medication(s) used.

If a heartworm, tick, or flea preventive program has been started, the times, dates, and the product used should be noted.

The pup's diet should be documented, including the quantity, brand name, and frequency of feeding.

Most breeders will have this information readily available, and probably more. Be sure you receive all of this information in writing. It is important to continue preventive health care, and without the health records, your veterinarian will be left guessing.

Papers

If the pup's parents are registered with the AKC, you should receive the puppy litter registration at the time you pay for the pup. There are exceptions to this rule. If you are buying a pet-quality pup, the breeder may withhold the registration papers until proof of neutering is furnished. If you pay for the pup in installments, papers may be retained until the final payment is received.

If AKC registration is not available from the breeder, you are in a buyer-beware situation. The AKC is not a regulatory agency. They can't get your money back, and you might need to resort to small-claims court for satisfaction. If you decide to buy the pup anyway, be sure to get a bill of sale from the breeder. This bill of sale should include the name and AKC registration numbers of the litter, sire,

Brittanys are excellent dogs for children.

When selecting a pup, check the sire's appearance as well as the dam's.

and dam, the dates of breeding, the date of whelping, and the names and phone numbers of the owners of both sire and dam.

A pedigree is a record of a few generations of the puppy's ancestors. It has no particular value for pets, but is very significant if you have purchased a competition dog and intend to breed it. If the breeder doesn't prepare a pedigree, one is always available from the AKC for a fee if you are able to furnish the AKC litter registration number or the permanent registration number of your new puppy.

If either you or the seller have negotiated any special terms that apply to the purchase, put them in writing. If you agree to spay or neuter the pup by a certain age, write it down. If the breeder guarantees the puppy to be in good health, get that in writing, together with the duration of the guarantee. Most breeders will replace a pup if it has a disease or deformity that is discovered by your veterinarian. The terms of the guarantee should clearly specify whether you receive your money back or you receive a replacement pup.

Taking Your Brittany Puppy Home

First Days in Your Home

When you have purchased your Brittany puppy, you must make certain adjustments in your lifestyle to accommodate this new family member. Depending on her age, Jill must be fed several meals per day at regular intervals. If she is kept in the house, she must be taken outside for eliminations. You must make allowances for Jill's exercise needs and include walks and playtimes in your daily plans. There are physical and emotional demands on your life that were not previously present.

Diet

The records you received with your Brittany should contain dietary information that lists the name of the food being fed, the frequency of meals, and the quantity that is being fed at each meal.

When you take Jill home, minimize the stress of environmental change by following the previously established feeding program. Even if you wish to change her diet to a better quality food, that change shouldn't be made immediately. After a week or two in your home, you can begin dietary changes if desired. Make those changes slowly by mixing the new product in gradually increasing amounts with the previous food. A total diet change should take at least a week, perhaps longer. Maintenance dietary recommendations are found in the chapter on feeding your Brittany on page 48.

Necessary Quarters

As a family pet, your new Brittany puppy is probably destined to spend much of her time inside your house. Perhaps you already have a fenced yard and expect her to have the run of the yard and sleep in your home at night. Those accommodations are fine, providing you have taken a few preliminary precautions to protect both your puppy and your property.

Kennel and Run

If your home provides for the construction of an outdoor kennel, choose an area that slopes gently downward from front to back. A few inches or even a foot of slope makes for good drainage away from the front of the run, where Jill will spend most of her time. That is particularly important if your home is in a rainy environment. A 6-foot (2 m) chain-link fence will serve your needs well. If possible, place the kennel in the shade of trees. Make the run as large as the space and your pocketbook will allow, and if you have a choice, make it longer than wide to allow for a maximum of exercise. Most kennels are not large enough to provide adequate exercise space for an athletic Brittany and should be used only as a place to safely house Jill when you are away. The run should be large enough to let Jill move about freely, and it should be located where shade from the sun is always available.

An elevated wooden platform that is large enough to allow your adult Brittany to stretch out should be built in a dry area. The platform should be high enough to keep the dog out of the mud, and if you live in an area where snow or rain prevails, it's best to put some type of cover over the platform to help keep it dry. If in hot, dry country, a sunscreen is essential.

Jill will also need a doghouse if she is to be an outdoor dog. Commercial molded fiberglass doghouses are available in sizes to fit a Brittany. Although expensive, they are usually a one-time investment. When shopping for a doghouse for a little puppy, it's sometimes difficult to remember that puppies grow up. Buy or build a house that won't be too small for a full-grown Brittany. The dome-shaped, igloo types and the conventional rectangular fiberglass houses both have removable bottoms for easy cleaning. The igloos are also insulated to be cool in the summer and to retain warmth in the winter.

There is one fact you must keep in mind: A kennel run may provide the opportunity for exercise, but it doesn't provide the initiative. It gives your pet a certain amount of freedom, but it's your responsibility to see that Jill gets the exercise she needs.

Naturally, if Jill sleeps in your home, elaborate outdoor housing is unnecessary. A word of caution: If your yard fence is only 3 feet (1 m) tall, it's probably not adequate to contain an energetic and adventuresome adult Brittany. A 3-foot fence is usually sufficient when the family is with the dog, but if left alone behind a short fence, boredom or loneliness may stimulate Jill to jump. Such a fence would be no challenge for a strong, athletic Brittany adult.

Crate Training

Many owners cringe at the thought of crating their Brittany. They can't imagine confining a sporting dog to a crate. If used properly, the crate is an excellent and harmless way to man-

A 3-foot fence is hardly a challenge for an athletic Brittany.

age your puppy. It can also be used in certain cases when Jill has reached adulthood, but you should never keep her in a crate for extended periods of time. Most dogs enjoy the safety and cave-like atmosphere of a crate when sleeping, and a crate often makes a dog a welcome guest in motel rooms when you are traveling.

Obtain a large fiberglass crate that has adequate ventilation. As in choosing a doghouse, don't make the mistake of buying a crate to fit a puppy. One day soon, Jill will grow up, and

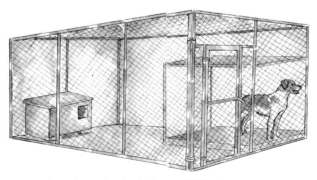

Be sure there is ample shade in your Brittany's run.

It is stressful to take a pup from his siblings before he is ready.

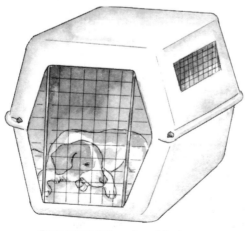

Pups appreciate a den of their own.

the crate must accommodate her then as well. Keep some article of your clothing or the puppy's favorite toy in the crate together with a blanket or rug. Confine Jill to the crate for short periods of time in the beginning, but always leave the crate open when it isn't being used.

When confining Jill to the crate, don't tease her. Crate her, walk away and pay no attention to her complaints. If she barks, respond with a sharp *"No,"* and continue with your work. Be sure to take her out of the crate frequently for eliminations.

Regular sessions of crating will result in acceptance of the crate as Jill's personal "den," and she will soon return there for naps or when the activity of the household becomes irritating. It will soon be a favorite place—one that is quiet and secluded.

A crate can be used instead of a wire pen or small room in which to confine her during housebreaking. It is also a great help when traveling and is preferable to a seat belt to control Jill in your car.

Never use the crate as a negative reinforcement in training. She should not be crated as punishment for doing something wrong. Give Jill some special treat when she enters the crate and another when she is taken out. If you make crating a positive experience, she won't resent it.

Bonding and Socialization

Human bonding and family adjustment occurs rapidly in a young Brittany puppy. During the brief period between three weeks and three months of age, Jill will form lifelong relationships with her human companions. If she is acquired before or during that time she will accept correction quickly and easily; the lessons offered will be promptly imprinted on her personality. This is the best time to establish your love and devotion to your new pet, and Jill will reciprocate.

As she becomes familiar with the household routine, Jill will quickly recognize the restrictions placed on her. Brittany puppies are amazingly tolerant of children, but young people should always be taught to handle the pup gently and rough play shouldn't be tolerated. Within a few weeks, Jill will be looking for ways to please you. Always playful, she will begin to learn to recognize her toys and to anticipate the ball games and hide and seek exercises. Worn out socks with a knot tied in them are excellent toys for a young Brittany. When Jill begins to mouth your hands, legs, or furniture, substitute a knotted sock and praise

A pen is furnished for the first few days in your home.

her as she carries it about. Have patience: Puppies do grow up!

Most new owners look forward to sharing the joys of puppyhood when they buy a Brittany. However, for the first few months, puppies require a great deal of personal attention and time commitment. The mischievous pup likes to play, chew, run, and romp with children or adults. She will grow like a weed, changing from a little ball of puppy fur to a gangly awkward teenager within a few weeks.

Watching the puppy mature, physically and mentally, is truly a wonderful experience, and your personal interaction during that period is essential. There's no doubt that a puppy adds something special to a family environment, but raising a Brittany puppy isn't a spectator sport. Responding to your care and attention, she learns the rules of the household. At the same time, you learn about Jill's character, her likes and dislikes, and the things that satisfy her the most. You can use this knowledge to great advantage when training is begun.

29

HOW-TO: Puppy-Proof Your Home

Many household chemicals are poisonous to pups.

Most healthy puppies are rather destructive little creatures, and Brittanys are no exception. Before you leave a puppy alone in your home for more than a few minutes, be sure to do a quick hazard inventory. Familiar objects that are safe for the family may present some degree of danger to a new puppy. Look around for some of the following puppy hazards.

• Low hanging telephone and computer cords make wonderful tug-of-war toys for a pup. Unfortunately, the wires may not hold up very well and may be difficult to replace. They are also dangerous should they become wrapped around Jill's neck.

• Drapes and curtains that swing at Jill's eye level are also quite challenging and may be attacked without provocation.

• Household electrical appliance cords are dangerous. They can cause mouth burns or electrical shock when chewed, and those that are accessible to the puppy should be unplugged

This phone cord will never be the same.

when Jill is left unsupervised, even for a few minutes.

• Cords that are unplugged but left hanging can also be dangerous for puppies. Dangling cords attached to irons, toasters, radios, and other appliances are prime targets for puppy attacks. An electric mixer and its contents smashed all over the kitchen floor is a hapless reminder that all cords should be coiled and put well out of Jill's reach.

• Household chemicals are sometimes accessible to an adventuresome pup. Items such as oven cleaner, laundry soap, bleach, dish washing soap, and insecticides, that are frequently kept beneath the kitchen sink are an ever-present danger to puppies.

• Scrubbers such as steel wool and plastic coils are, for whatever reason, attractive to puppies and may be chewed up and swallowed. Sponges are particularly hazardous. They are attractive to pups, and if swallowed, may require surgical removal.

In case Jill does get into a cupboard, try to ascertain what objects or chemicals may have been swallowed, read the labels, contact your veterinarian, and watch the pup carefully for signs of illness such as lethargy, vomiting, and diarrhea.

• Houseplants are another attractive target for puppies to attack. Plant dangers are three-fold. First, most potted plants can't defend themselves against a puppy encounter and usually lose the conflict and their lives. Second, messy, damp potting soil, mixed with shreds of leaves, stems, and roots,

Although a sponge looks harmless, it can be serious if swallowed.

spread all over the floor isn't a pretty sight. And third, some common house and garden plants are poisonous and can cause serious illnesses in dogs. (See the list of plants that are poisonous to dogs at right.)

• Although not usually poisonous, artificial foliage may upset Jill's stomach, resulting in vomiting and diarrhea. The gastric upset is usually self-limiting and easily treated, but the clean-up chore isn't pleasant.

• Low bookshelves might look like a potpourri of leather and paper toys to Jill. Books are expensive chew toys for pups and should be protected.

• Because children's rooms often contain foam rubber balls, plastic toys, seashells, dolls, and other gimcracks and gewgaws, it's a good idea to keep

the doors to those rooms closed to keep your puppy out. A small sponge rubber jacks ball may look harmless enough, but a Brittany puppy may swallow it without much effort. The ball may not go through the pyloric opening of the stomach into the small intestine, and unless it is retrieved quickly, it can require surgical removal.

• Tablecloths, doilies, and coffee table scarves that hang over the tables' edges may be tug-of-war targets for your new Brittany pup.

• Throw rugs, especially those with tassels, also provide great fun and entertainment for mischievous Jill.

• If Jill is to spend much time in the house, put up a couple of infant gates on doorways to limit her roaming to one or two rooms. A portable dog pen will serve the same purpose and can be moved from room to room. Crating the pup is another way to

Poisonous Plants
• azaleas
• castor bean
• corn cockle
• English holly berries
• foxglove
• Jerusalem cherry
• jessamine
• jimson weed
• milkweed
• mistletoe
• oleander
• philodendron
• rattlebox
• rhododendron
• water hemlock

protect and control her for the first few weeks in your home.

Puppy-proofing a house isn't easy; sometimes it's impossible. Perhaps the best way to save your valuables from destruction is to confine the young puppy to the yard or provide a safe, attractive play area in the garage.

Besides the mess, this pup will probably be sick if he finishes eating the plant.

If puppies don't have siblings to chew on they chew on whatever is available.

A Brittany Puppy in Your Yard

If you have a fenced yard, the puppy-proofing tasks are easier, but don't relax until you have once again done a hazard inventory. Your fence may be inadequate; if constructed of wood, it is chewable. If it doesn't extend into the ground several inches, it may only serve to teach Jill to dig out.

Garden hoses may be attacked and punctured if they are not kept out of reach of the venturesome little Brittany. Gardening chemicals such as fertilizers and insecticides present major problems to pups. Jill may chew on a bag, box, or sprayer hose, and ingest toxic chemicals. All such products should be put well out of reach of your new Brittany.

Fertilizers and insecticides that have been recently applied to the lawn or garden should be watered well into the soil to prevent Jill from contami-

nating her feet and then licking the toxins off. Tiny amounts of such poisons can cause seizures in young pups, and repeated exposure may cause similar problems in adults. When watering the lawn after the application of chemicals, be sure that Jill doesn't drink from pools or puddles that form on sidewalks. Keep dogs off treated lawns for 48 hours!

Labels on the packages tell you of the danger of garden products. If your pup has chewed and possibly consumed the contents, call your veterinarian immediately. Provide the label ingredients and the amount consumed, if it can be ascertained. Don't attempt to treat the puppy on your own unless efforts to obtain professional help fail. Keep in mind that your puppy is quite small and has a rapid metabolic rate; that makes the danger even greater, and the need to get immediate professional help more urgent.

Antifreeze should be kept out of reach because it has a sweet taste that dogs usually like. It contains a kidney toxin that may kill your dog, and unfortunately, treatment is not very effective even when the poisoning is discovered early. This isn't just a puppy problem, but can affect adults of all species as well. In the event that antifreeze poisoning is suspected, seek professional help immediately. If Jill has access to the garage, keep the floor and driveway clean and free from engine fluids that may drip from your car.

Windshield washer fluid and other alcohol-containing products are equally dangerous. Virtually all automotive chemicals may be extremely hazardous to Jill's health. Don't leave oils, greases, or other products where she can reach them.

Paint, turpentine, thinner, and acetone should be stored well out of the dog's reach. Paint removers are particularly dangerous, and even a quick investigative lick can cause severe tongue burns. A clumsy puppy might tip a can over while looking for something to do, soaking its feet with the caustic stuff. If this happens, rinse the feet immediately with gallons of cool water and then wash them off with soap and water and call your veterinarian.

Swimming pools can also be hazardous to your new Brittany. Brittanys are excellent swimmers, but some pools are constructed with escape ladders that only humans can use. If you have such a pool, provide a means of escape for your dog before she is allowed to come in contact with the pool. Show Jill where the steps are and teach her how to use them.

If the foregoing discussion gives you the impression that Brittany puppies are animated, relentless, destructive

When Brittanys are hunting, they require the best nutrition.

forces please understand that these are worst-case scenarios. Brittany puppies are no worse than any other pups, and most Brittany youngsters are not intent on destruction. All puppies are subject to mischievous activities that land them in trouble once in a while. By identifying hazards, you might save your puppy's life or at least save yourself some money.

Antifreeze is a deadly poison to dogs.

Exercise

Brittanys thrive on regular exercise. They are athletic sporting dogs that are easily bored if they have nothing to do. Exercise tends to keep puppies out of mischief and produces solid musculature in growing youths. Exercise continues to be important throughout life. It helps condition adults, keeping them in prime hunting condition. Exercise also tends to minimize the effects of aging conditions such as arthritis. Obesity can be combated through an exercise and diet program.

If you have a large fenced yard, Jill will no doubt initiate and play some games by herself, but don't rely on self-imposed exercise. When children of the family are available to romp and play with their Brittany friend, lack of exercise is rarely a problem. If Jill is kept indoors or in a kennel run, you are obliged to help her exercise. Play sessions, jogging, or regular, frequent long walks will fulfill her exercise needs.

If your lifestyle doesn't allow you to spend time exercising your energetic companion, consider a more sedentary pet.

Pups always chew your best shoes if allowed.

Chewing

Brittanys are happy, active puppies with active mouths; like all puppies, they are prone to chewing. A puppy's attraction to an item seems to be directly proportional to the replacement cost of that item. A child's favorite toy or your most expensive gloves are the ones that suffer the most abuse. For some unknown reason, old, wornout shoes aren't as likely to be chewed as new ones. Shoes should never be used as toys under any circumstances. If allowed, Jill will pass right by a rawhide chewstick and pick up an expensive shoe.

Chewing is programmed into the makeup of all puppies, but Brittanys learn easily, and you shouldn't be discouraged from obtaining a young pup. You should realize that your lifestyle will be affected by a new puppy's presence. You should accept the challenge to pick up your personal belongings and store them out of reach of the pup. Children should be taught to pick up their toys and clothes at the same time that you are training Jill to play with her own toys.

Brittanys thrive on attention, and it is easy to channel their chewing to appropriate objects. Chewing is a habit that is usually only corrected by substitution. A stern vocal reprimand should accompany each shoe-chewing episode. Immediately following the reprimand, offer Jill some attractive and appropriate toy such as a rawhide bone, knotted sock, or chewstick.

Automobiles

We hope that your Brittany's only association with cars will be as a backseat passenger. Far too many dogs are injured while following their owners' automobiles, chasing neighbor's cars, or running into street traffic. Few dogs suffer any great fear of riding in cars. If the engine noise or the vehicle's movement frightens Jill, patience and short trips will gradually condition her to the engine noise and movement.

It is important to make your Brittany behave while riding in a car, whether or not she is afraid. You decide where you want Jill to ride and insist that she stay in the designated area. Pet supply stores have dog safety harnesses that fasten into an automobile's seat belt system and hold the pet in a fairly confined area of the car. They are good insurance.

If you travel with your Brittany, a crate should be used whenever space allows. It is the safest and most positive means of confinement, but please don't put your Brittany in a crate in the car's trunk!

Motion sickness is always a messy business. Carsickness causes signs of abdominal distress such as nausea, salivation, and vomiting. If Jill suffers from this malady, your veterinarian or the drugstore can furnish some motion sickness tablets. The dosage varies according to the size and age of the dog, and although most are relatively safe, you should check the product dosage with your veterinarian. In time, most dogs outgrow the problem, but until then, give a dose of the drug about an hour before your car trip. Jill will appreciate it, and it beats cleaning up the mess afterward.

Another precaution you can take to avoid carsickness is to withhold all feed for two hours before an automobile trip. Save the food until after the ride. During a day of activity, Jill can be fed a high-protein paste dietary supplement instead of bulky dog food. These products are available at most pet stores or veterinary offices and provide dietary supplementation without the bulk of regular dog foods.

If you drive a pickup truck, you may be tempted to allow your Brittany to ride in the back. Fight the urge! If you cannot resist, then at least cross-tie Jill so it is impossible for her to leave the moving vehicle. Then prepare to periodically consult a veterinarian about Jill's eyes that will no doubt suffer abuse from the dust and debris that is flying about.

Boarding Kennels

When you first acquire your puppy, you should locate a place for her to stay when you can't be home to care for her. If you have constructed a kennel run in your yard, ask a trustworthy neighbor or friend to care for Jill there. That person should naturally make friends with Jill before taking the responsibility for her care. Don't let her stay in a backyard kennel for extended periods of time with no one to check on her appetite, drinking water, and health.

Check with the person who raised your puppy. Sometimes breeders have facilities to keep your dog for a time. Settle on the least crowded and most secure boarding facility you can find.

Commercial boarding kennels present stress-related health risks to the dogs boarded therein. Family pets resent being confined to small areas; some become bored with inactivity and others are frightened or challenged by the commotion and barking of their kennelmates. Diet changes add to the stress of kenneled dogs. The odors of females in heat are unnerving to intact males.

Some boarding kennels are spotless and well managed, but unfortunately, many are not. Boarding kennels may be a source of fleas, ticks, lice, and other external parasites. Although less likely, inadequate cleaning may also predispose your Brittany to intestinal parasite infestation. The most common complaint resulting from a stay in a boarding facility is *kennel cough*, which is manifested by a chronic, deep, croupy, honking cough that lasts for weeks after the pet returns home.

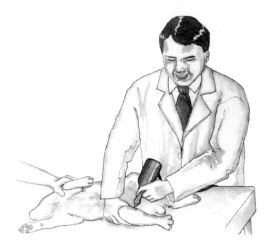

Tattoo your social security number in the pup's flank.

Veterinary Care

A visit to your veterinarian is strongly advised when you acquire a new puppy, even if your Brittany seems to be in perfect health. The veterinarian will advise you on the appropriate timing of future booster vaccinations, as well as other preventive health measures that will guard your pet's health.

New animal-health ideas and products are introduced frequently in veterinary medicine. Research information may reveal better ways of immunizing dogs, treating or controlling parasites, preventing heartworm infestations, or detecting diseases.

Identification

Tattoos and Microchips

Even in the best-regulated households, puppies sometimes manage to wander off. Jill should be permanently identified as early as possible. This may be achieved by tattooing some identifying numbers or letters on her flank or in her ear. A microchip may be implanted under her skin to provide further identification. Your veterinarian will advise you of the available means of identification and will help implement your choice.

No form of protection is effective, however, unless you have the identification registered with an animal relocation program. The AKC maintains a 24-hour hotline "Home Again" service. You can register Jill's tattoo or microchip number with this service. The cost is minimal, and your veterinarian, pet supply store, or the AKC can provide you with a registration form. A humane society, shelter, or purebred rescue organization can scan for the microchip or look for a flank or ear tattoo. It is the owner's responsibility to notify the Home Again registry of address or phone number changes.

If you can't avoid boarding Jill in a commercial kennel, visit and tour the facility before you need it. If a tour is denied, you are in the wrong kennel. If allowed to walk through the boarding facility, look for sick animals, and signs of diarrhea, vomiting, coughing, or sneezing.

If possible, locate a kennel that specializes in boarding sporting dogs, a kennel in which each dog has its own private indoor space that is connected to a large outdoor run. The best type of facility will have runs that are separated from one another by block or brick walls instead of wire fencing. Such an arrangement will minimize conflict with neighbor dogs and will also slightly reduce the probability of exposure to respiratory infections.

Responsible boarding kennels require proof of a variety of inoculations prior to boarding your dog. Be pleased when you locate such a facility, and be prepared to have Jill's vaccination records available to be copied to the kennel files.

Permanent identification will help ensure that your dog finds its way back home.

Name Tags

Tags are available through any pet supply shop. Order one with your name, address, and telephone number, and attach it securely to Jill's collar. The best type of identification tag is one that rivets flatly to the web or leather collar. This type comes complete with rivets, and no special application equipment is needed. If necessary, a saddle shop or shoe repairperson will rivet the tag flat against the collar for a nominal fee. This type of tag can't be easily lost and isn't likely to hang on limbs,

underbrush, or fences. Never allow your puppy outside without your name and address attached. If nothing better is possible, print your name and telephone number with waterproof ink on the pup's nylon web collar.

Dogs are commonly lost when their owners are gone from home and cannot be reached by telephone. If friends are watching your dog while you are on vacation, print their name and phone number in waterproof ink on a piece of gray duct tape and wrap it on Jill's collar.

Training Your Brittany

Housebreaking

Brittanys are naturally clean dogs, and many will housebreak themselves if given the opportunity. Housebreaking is a subject that should be discussed, even if your dog lives outside most of the time.

Young puppies use little discretion, and when they feel the urge to urinate or defecate, they do it. The job is finished before you notice; then it's too late to correct. A professional dog trainer has estimated that to be effective, your response to Chip's "accident" must occur within five seconds from the time it happens. After that time the puppy will not associate his action with any corrective measure you may take. Remember that to the untrained pup, urinating or defecating isn't a mistake, it isn't an accident, it's natural, and it's done without thought.

The first rule is to always take Chip to a designated area of the yard for his eliminations. Once the odors of previous eliminations are established in the toilet area, the pup will seek out that spot when necessary. Take him to the toilet area immediately after each meal, when he wakes in the morning, after naps, and before bedtime at night. If you are able to train yourself to that task, the pup will be housebroken before you know it.

For the first week or so, don't let Chip out of your sight when he is indoors. Each time he squats to urinate or defecate, say *"No,"* in a normal tone of voice and then pick him up and carry him to the toilet area in the yard. Even if he has started to urinate or defecate, he should be carried outside to finish. Don't allow him to finish on the floor and then take him outside—this will only train Chip to take a trip to the backyard after his elimination. After he has emptied his bladder or bowel in the toilet area, praise him, play with him for a moment, and then allow him back inside.

Don't use a negative approach to housebreaking. A pup has no way of knowing about human customs or habits until he is taught. It is a serious error to punish, scold, or reprimand a puppy for messing on the floor. If you swat Chip when he is performing a natural act, you will confuse him. Rubbing his nose in his urine is equally confusing to the pup and isn't likely to make a lasting impression on him. Once the act of urination or defecation is completed, it's gone from the animal's mind. Remember the five-second rule.

Prevention, substitution, and positive reinforcement are the most reliable tools to use in housebreaking your pup.

• *Prevent* him from messing on the floor by confining him to a pen or crate; never let him out of your sight while in the house.

• *Substitute* the toilet area of the yard for your carpet. When he shows signs of turning in circles in preparation for eliminating the bowel, pick him up quickly and get him outside.

• *Praise and reward* him when he complies and deposits his eliminations in the appropriate place. Great patience is required to housebreak a pup, and persistence will pay off.

Trainers often advise attaching a bell on a string inside the back door. It isn't uncommon for a 12-week-old Brittany to learn to ring the bell to go outside. Teaching the pup to use the bell is easy. The pup is first taken to the door, the bell is rung with his foot, and then he is put outside and amply rewarded.

During Chip's housebreaking, pick up his food and water at least a couple of hours before bedtime and confine him in a crate or small pen during the night. If he fusses, you must get out of bed and take him to his toilet area. This is a fundamental concept of training; his fussing means a trip to the toilet. It doesn't mean attention, playtime, or food.

Finally, don't try to reason with a nine-week-old puppy. You can explain why he should always go outside, but you will never make him understand. Brittanys are intelligent dogs, but their reasoning powers are not easily engaged at this early age.

Paper Training

Paper training isn't recommended, except for specific situations. If you must leave Chip inside the house by himself for extended periods of time, paper training might be warranted. When you find it necessary to paper train a pup, obtain a portable dog pen and confine the pup to the pen all the time that you aren't with him. Cover half the floor of the pen with a dozen or so sheets of newspaper, and use the other half of the pen for his food and water dishes, bed, and toys. In all probability Chip will use the paper-covered area for eliminations right away. Always clean up his messes as soon as they are seen.

After a few days, the pen can be removed while you are at home, but leave the papers in the same spot. When the pup is running free in the house and stops to urinate, rush him to the papers and reward him when he uses them. Eventually he will seek out and use the papers for his eliminations.

Collar and Leash Training

Like housebreaking, collar and leash training is a fundamental part of good manners that all dogs should learn. Although there are many methods of training a dog to walk on a leash, a positive approach should always be taken. A Brittany puppy is an easy subject. Chip will want to follow you anyway and adding a collar and leash doesn't put much stress on his little body and mind.

A leather buckle collar or nylon web collar is available in the correct size at the pet supply store. It should be snug, but not tight. When investing in a buckle collar for a young pup, buy one large enough to allow for growth. Your new pup should be introduced to his collar as soon as possible, but for the

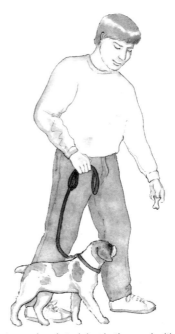

Start your leash training in the yard without an audience.

It only takes a few days for the pup to get used to the collar.

first two or three days, the collar shouldn't be left on Chip when he is alone. Later, when he is no longer

This pup is ready for housebreaking.

troubled by the collar's presence, it is safe to leave it on him all the time. Choke collars should always be used for training, but for elementary leash work in young puppies, a web collar is fine.

Snap a leash about 4 to 6 feet (1.5–2 m) long onto the collar and let Chip drag it while you add encouragement by offering him a tidbit now and then. Then pick up the leash and take another short walk around the yard. In the beginning, it's best to take only a few steps at a time, coaxing Chip to follow by offering tidbits from your fingers. The pup will soon connect his rewards with the training, and Chip will welcome the appearance of his leash each day. Although it is important to let the puppy know who has control of the leash, it should be done in a positive way, never as a punishment or correction.

Flexible, lightweight leashes of various strengths and lengths that retract into a plastic handle may be purchased in a pet-supply store. They are convenient and offer your dog more freedom than standard leashes. They may be used after Chip has become accustomed to walking on lead, but should not be used during his training period.

Once the pup has begun to accept the leash, you can exercise Chip out of his yard, and the new experiences, smells, and sights are ample reward for the restriction of the collar and leash. Don't begin serious obedience training at first; for a week or two just enjoy the companionship of your new pup.

From that easy beginning you can gradually progress to teaching the pup to walk on your left side, in preparation for more advanced training. As Chip grows, the buckle collar should be replaced with a larger size, and it should be left on him at all times for identification.

Advanced Training

Basic obedience training is mandatory if you intend to take Chip on walks with you. When training is approached gently and positively, and in short sessions, it is a rewarding experience.

Don't be discouraged when Chip becomes obstinate, sits down, drags his feet, and refuses to listen or cooperate. Have patience; take your time. What isn't learned today will be learned tomorrow. Others have done this, certainly you can do it too.

Hopefully, when you begin, the pup will have already accepted his leash. Remove the web or leather collar and put a choke collar in its place, snap on the sturdy nylon web leash, and begin the first exercise.

A pair of happy Brittanys.

Choke Collar

A choke collar should always be used for training. This piece of equipment is misnamed if it used correctly. It is formed from a short piece of smooth chain or strong nylon fabric with a ring fastened to each end. In order to work properly, it should be fitted to the dog. One size won't fit your Brittany from puppyhood to adulthood. It should measure approximately 2 inches (5.1 cm) greater than the circumference of the dog's neck. Most Brittanys respond equally well to either nylon or chain collars.

To form the collar, drop the chain (or fabric) through one of the rings. Then attach the lead-snap to the free ring. Place the collar on the dog so that the end of the collar that is attached to the leash comes up the left side of the dog and crosses from left to right over the top of his neck. Chip is maintained on your left side, and when it is necessary to correct the dog's action, the collar is given a quick tug and then released. If a choke collar is placed on the dog's neck incorrectly, it will not release quickly and may injure him. A choke collar that is too long will not close quickly enough to be effective. Keep in mind that the foregoing discussion assumes that the dog will be walking on your left side.

Be sure the choke collar is put on properly.

Pronged Collars

Training collars are available that are made of a dozen or so hinged wire prongs. The dull prongs turn against the dog's neck when the leash is tightened. They may be an effective way of training an unruly dog, but rarely if ever are they needed on a Brittany. They should be used only by professional trainers (if necessary), and when used, must never be abused. If you need a pronged collar to control your Brittany, you probably don't need the dog. Prong collars are banned from the premises of AKC shows.

Command Clarity

Separate every command into five parts and make each part clear and distinct. Chip has better hearing than you do, so shouting isn't going to add anything positive to the training. Neither should the command be repeated time and again for a single function.

First, say the dog's *name* clearly. This is difficult when his name is complex or lengthy, so if necessary, shorten the name and make it simple. When you say *"Chip,"* you'll get his attention; that lets him know that you will soon give a command that you

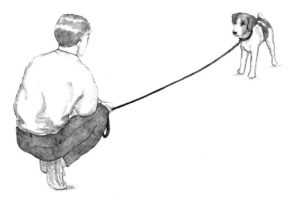

It's easy to teach a pup to come, because it's what he wants to do anyway.

expect to be followed. After a delay of a second or two, give the *command.* After another few seconds, *enforce* the action, gently and firmly. After the action has been successfully performed, *release* him from the command and offer a *reward* with your praise.

It is best to schedule training sessions before mealtimes and to use small treats to encourage the pup. Positive reinforcement and encouragement will always convince a puppy to follow your commands.

Come

This is perhaps the easiest command to teach your puppy and can be used in many everyday situations and games. You will probably teach your pup to *"Come"* at feeding time, and the pup won't realize what you are doing. This is one exercise that can be learned by a young pup and the sooner it is mastered the better. It should be practiced until Chip's response is automatic.

Fasten a long lightweight nylon line to Chip's collar. Allow him to wander away from you for some distance. Then, with zeal, drop to one knee and give the command, *"Chip,* (hesitation) *come."* If Chip doesn't respond with the enthusiasm you expect, give a tug or two on the line, repeating the command. When Chip arrives on your lap, lavish praise on him and give him a tidbit. Then release him from the exercise with an *"OK,"* and continue to praise him.

Repeat this exercise frequently at odd times to catch him off guard. When his response to the command has become automatic, try him off leash, in the fenced yard. Repeat the command several times daily for grooming, feeding, and especially for petting.

Never call your dog to you to scold or discipline him. That will defeat your purpose. Instead, each time he comes on command, praise and pet him, regardless of what mischief you have called him away from.

Sit

With your puppy at your left side, in a calm, normal voice, say *"Chip."* Wait a second before you say *"Sit,"* and when that command has been absorbed, push the pup's bottom to the ground. To let the dog understand exactly what you desire, it's important to allow a few seconds after the *sit* command is given before the action is taken. Chip must associate the command with the desired action. As you enforce the *sit* command, offer a tidbit to the dog at eye level, immediately in front of and very close to his muzzle. This will encourage him to sit and stay in that position. After a few seconds of sitting, release him by saying, *"OK,"* then praise him.

The tidbit reward is only used in the beginning of any training; praise and petting is the real reward for both of you. Acclamation must be given in abundance after the correct performance of each exercise. When the pup doesn't perform the exercise correctly, don't make a big issue of the error; use the word *"Wrong,"* in a conversational tone, before you make the correction. Reserve the word *no*, and a gruff voice, for times when Chip is in trouble, and you want him to refrain from whatever mischief he is involved in.

Practice the sitting exercise several times a day, but don't expect miracles! If you're lucky, the dog will catch on the first day, but don't count on it. Don't add to his confusion with more training at this time.

In the next session, practice the *sit* command several times, and if met with success, progress to another exercise. If it takes several sessions to learn to *sit* correctly, so be it. You are in no hurry, and some dogs take longer than others. Ten-week-old puppies have short attention spans and aren't

The pup must be helped to sit *the first few times.*

usually as quick to learn or remember simple exercises as older dogs.

Stay

When your Brittany has mastered sitting and is looking for his tidbit, tell him to *"Stay,"* while you remain standing at his right side. Present your outstretched palm in front of his muzzle as you give the *stay* command. If he tries to lie down or stand up, tell him *"Wrong,"* repeat the command *"Stay,"* and put him back into a sitting position. After a few seconds, release him from the stay with an *"OK,"* and give him a reward. Again, the command is broken into several parts. First, the dog's name, then the command, then the action, the release, and finally, the reward and praise.

A beautiful Brittany posing for the camera.

The next step is to move away from Chip while he is obeying the *stay* command. When you put the leash on the ground and start to walk away, the faithful pup will try to follow. Say *"Wrong,"* repeat the *stay* command, place Chip in the sitting position, display your outstretched flat palm and

Down is more difficult for a dog to understand.

back away again. After a few tries, the pup will get the idea and stay-put while you take several steps backward, away from him. Then you must return to his side to finish the exercise. Don't forget to release him from the stay and never finish the exercise without praise and a reward.

One word of caution: Don't expect too much from a puppy. Take only a few steps away in the beginning. Don't push Chip to the limit and expect him to stay interminably like well-trained dogs in obedience trials. Return quickly to his side, take your position with the dog on your left, pick up the leash, and release him from the stay command. In the beginning, most pups are doing well if they stay for 20 seconds without fidgeting.

Down

This command is used in obedience trials and is also a convenient way to let the pup relax while you talk to neighbors on your daily walks. It should be given in the same way that the *sit* command is used. Begin the exercise with the dog in the sitting or standing position. Be sure to hesitate between the dog's name and the command. *"Chip, (hesitation) down,"* is the command. Don't muddy the issue with excess words. Never tell the dog to *lie down* or confuse the puppy even more with *"Chip, Sit Down."*

After you have given the *down* command, push his body to the ground, slowly and gently. Don't fight him. If necessary, hold a tidbit so low that he can't reach it without lying down. Or, if he doesn't cooperate, push him to the sitting position, and fold his elbows, placing his belly against the ground.

After the *down* command comes the inevitable *stay*, that is accompanied by walking away a few steps. Finish the exercise by returning to him, releasing him from the exercise,

A picture-perfect pointing stance.

and lauding great praise on him. Once the pup realizes that you aren't leaving him, and if he stays you will return with more praise and tidbits, he will be happy to cooperate.

Off

This is another logical and valuable command for Chip to learn. *Off* means to get off the furniture, to get his feet off the windowsill, or to stop jumping on a person, another dog, or any other object. It tells the dog to stop what he is doing and place all four feet on the ground. It is taught in much the same way as any other command, except that you must wait until the appropriate moment to use the command to make the lesson meaningful.

Heel

Your Brittany is now familiar with the leash and doesn't panic when you

occasionally tug on it. Chip realizes that each time you bring out his leash, a walk is on the morning's agenda and new vistas are about to be discovered.

These curious pups have uncovered some wild game.

45

or behind you, but don't allow him to bolt ahead. If he does move past your left knee, do an "about face," reverse and walk in the opposite direction. Say *"Chip, heel"* as you make that turn. Soon Chip will watch where you put your left foot and keep his body in line with you.

After he has properly *heeled* for a dozen steps, stop, and push his bottom to the ground to the sitting position as you give the *sit* command. Then release him with an *"OK,"* reward him with a tidbit and praise, and begin the exercise again.

Heeling is fine for dog shows and for maximum control of your dog in a crowd, and it is essential when crossing busy streets. That's where heeling should end; it is boring for Chip, and although all dogs should learn to heel, they should be given more freedom whenever the situation and space will allow. At this time a flexible lead may be introduced to allow Chip more freedom to investigate.

Leads and collars may be compared to suits of clothing. The choke collar, whether chain or fabric, tells Chip that you intend to maintain maximum control. He will expect obedience work or training. The web collar becomes everyday wear, with or without a leash. The web collar and short leash tells him that this is to be a fun time or a controlled walk. A flexible lead and web collar or no lead means a romp in the park.

Innate and Learned Behavior

It is the nature of a dog to avoid soiling its living space. To teach a dog to use a certain area of the yard is simply expanding on its natural tendencies to separate its den from its eliminations. A Brittany is a natural retriever and will probably retrieve from puppyhood without training. Other training, however, is not that easy. You must supersede what is natural for the dog in order to cause your pet to honor your desires. It is natural for a dog

Heel *is only used in obedience trials, in crowds, or when crossing the street.*

Heeling is another exercise that all well-behaved dogs should learn. Place Chip on your left side, running the leash through your left hand, holding it with your right. Give him the command, *"Chip, sit."* Then as you step off with your left foot, give the command, *"Heel."* As you walk along, keep Chip walking with his nose by your left knee with gentle tugs on the leash.

If he wants to lag behind, encourage him to keep up with you by teasing him along with a tidbit held in your right hand. Soon he will be walking by your side, taking turns and stops in his stride.

This is a tough exercise for an ambitious puppy to master. Chip is anxious to forge ahead and investigate something at the far end of his leash. Keep the leash short, but don't hold it too tightly. At first, leave slack enough for him to move a step ahead to run free, but such exercises as walking on a leash, sitting, heeling, or staying are learned behaviors.

All pups, but especially Brittanys, are active, inquisitive, and energetic; they sometimes misbehave. Don't make a federal case out of each mistake. It is natural for them to play and have fun. As a teacher, you should always try to make their education as painless as possible. No training exercises should take more than a couple of minutes. If continued for too long, Chip will become bored and lose interest. Change frequently from one exercise to another, and don't forget to play with the pup in between exercises.

Take your time, don't forget the rewards, and always end the training sessions with playtime. Don't expect the pup to be ready for an obedience ring at the end of the first week.

Never use negative reinforcement when attempting early training. Don't spank or scold a pup that is guilty of nothing more than bouncing up when he should be sitting. It is the pup's nature to remember the spanking, but he might forget what action on his part precipitated the punishment.

Repeat the training that you have started every day or if that isn't possible, repeat it several times a week. Playing is natural but sitting, staying, and heeling are learned behaviors. Training must be continued and repeated in order to fix the learned behavior in his mind and make it automatic.

Feeding Your Brittany

A Brittany's appearance, ability, and stamina are directly related to the quantity and quality of its food. Any discussion of canine nutrition should begin with one simple fact: If something looks too good to be true, it probably is. A dog food that costs pennies is usually worth about what it costs. You can't package dollars worth of nutrition in a bag and sell it for a few cents. Considering the time and expense that you have spent on your Brittany, dog food is a poor place to economize.

Dry food should be bought in quantities that correspond to the number of dogs you are feeding, and it should be stored in airtight containers. Dog food is less expensive in 50-pound bags, but unless it is used quickly, storage can cause the loss of nutrients when the food is exposed to the air. Fats may become rancid, and vitamins A, D, E, K, and some B complex may be lost. For that same reason, beware of buying dry dog food from stores that have low product inventory turnover.

Preservatives and additives that protect against early oxidation maintain the palatability of dry foods. Some foods are preserved with natural antioxidants such as vitamin C and E and contain no artificial preservatives. Look for these foods; they're often the best. Don't store bagged dog food in warm places because elevated temperatures enhance deterioration of the ingredients.

Types of Foods Available

Canned Foods

Three types of dog foods are presently available. Many companies produce all three. Canned foods are expensive, but they store well and are highly palatable. Feeding canned food alone may not give Jill an adequate amount of roughage in her diet and may predispose her to urinary frequency. Canned food is more than 60 percent water and has preservatives that may cause a diuretic effect when fed exclusively. The meat contained in canned dog foods often isn't of the highest quality in spite of what dog food commercials would have you believe.

Semi-moist Foods

Soft-moist or semi-moist foods that are sold in sealed packets are also are quite palatable, but they don't store as

These puppies require good nutrition for growing.

Besides exercise, athletic dogs require good nutrition.

well as canned foods. They look like hamburger or other ground meat and sell well because of their appearance. They are expensive and contain rather large amounts of sugar and some questionable chemical preservatives that are not found in dry foods.

The biggest problem encountered when feeding semi-moist foods is the water consumption that seems to accompany their use. A dog that is fed this type of food exclusively usually will drink large quantities of water, resulting in frequent urination. Semi-moist foods are also occasionally incriminated as the cause of certain allergic reactions.

Dry Foods

Dry dog foods are usually the least expensive and easiest to feed. Bal-anced nutrition is possible for a sporting dog using dry food exclusively, but all dry foods are not the same; they vary greatly in nutritional content and palatability. You shouldn't need to flavor a dry food to get a healthy dog to eat it, and you shouldn't need to add supplements to a dry dog food to make it complete and balanced.

Varieties of Dry Food

There are three general varieties of dry dog foods: generic, commercial, and premium.

Premium Brands

Premium brands are usually the most expensive dry dog foods on the market. They are sold in veterinary hospitals and pet supermarkets, and most of them are well accepted by

Choose dog food intelligently, not by advertisements.

dogs. Generally, premium dry dog foods contain adequate nutrition, require no supplementation, and have sufficient taste to suit even the most finicky appetites. In many cases, premium dry dog foods may be fed free choice, meaning that the food is left out so the dog has access to it at all times, to be eaten whenever desired. Naturally that is not an option if your Brittany is a glutton.

To increase palatability, a basic diet of complete and balanced dry food can be mixed with a premium canned food.

Commercial Brands

Commercial dry dog foods are those that are found stacked on the shelves of grocery stores, supermarkets, and discount stores. Many of these products provide excellent nutrition, and some of the name brands have found their place in the market for decades. That alone is an indication that they are more than adequate for the average canine pet. Any discussion of these commercial foods must be broad, because they vary greatly in quality. In order to be sure of your selection, contact the manufacturer and ask for the data on the food being considered. You should receive a report on feeding trials being conducted, the sources of all the ingredients, and the analysis.

Generic Brands

When shopping, always consider generic brands; but before buying, be sure they conform to the standards discussed in this section. The biggest problem with generic foods is that they may vary in composition from month to month, as various grains or other ingredients become more or less available. Generic foods are rarely subjected to feeding trials because of the expense of those trials.

Always note the turnover or popularity of a dog food before purchasing it. Ask the department manager which food is restocked most frequently then read the label, check the ingredients, and make your purchase.

Dog Food Labels

If the package of dog food you are planning to buy doesn't plainly list its composition, pick another product. Dog foods containing the best ingredients and balanced nutritional elements will proudly display that information.

All dog foods are not equal. Read package labels; call or write to manufacturers. Know what you are feeding Jill! To buy a dog food because it is low priced or because the total protein is higher than other brands makes no more sense than choosing a food by the picture on a bag. The *sources* and *quality* of protein, carbohydrate, and fat are as important as the quantities. Always think of ingredient quality as well as quantity.

Don't base your selection on television ads. These ads typically show a beautiful litter of puppies, a happy companion dog, or a group of "winning dogs." Those paid actors are marketing tools, and they may or may not be promoting a superior dog food.

Some labels state that the dog food meets the recommendations of the National Research Council. That statement may apply only to canine maintenance requirements, and the food should be adequate for pets under minimal stress. For growing puppies, competition dogs, or breeding animals, maintenance foods may not be acceptable because they don't supply the increased energy demands of work, training, growth, pregnancy, or lactation.

Labels may specify the quantities of available nutrients but not the *bioavailable* nutrients (that is the amount of the food that can actually be used by a dog for its energy requirements). If an essential element is fed to a dog in a form that is not bioavailable, it might as well be left on the store shelf.

Always look for the source of protein. The ingredient list should give you that information. Vegetable protein sources such as corn or soy flour may provide an excellent analysis on the package, but it may be misleading if that protein is not bioavailable.

Feeding Trials

You will find foods with label declarations that they have passed the *American Association of Feed Control Officials* (AAFCO) feeding trials for the entire lifecycle of canines. You can generally rest assured that products so labeled contain the right amount of bioavailable food elements required for puppies, youths, and adults.

If the AAFCO declaration is not shown, get a phone number from the package and call the manufacturer. Obtain feeding trial results. Ask about the sources of protein and fat. Request information about the formulation of the products, and ask if the formula is kept constant, regardless of the seasonal variation of ingredient costs.

If you are unable to obtain the desired information about a product, choose another brand. If unable to understand information provided by manufacturers, consult with your veterinarian. If she or he isn't able to help you make the decision, borrow a text on the subject. Most veterinary clinics have reference sources for nutritional requirements of dogs.

Nutritional Elements

Water

Fresh drinking water must be supplied to Jill for all of her life. Other nutritional elements may be varied under different circumstances, but a source of clean water is always essential. That doesn't mean adding water to a dirty pan. Like humans, dogs prefer cool, fresh water in a clean pan.

Protein

Amino acids (protein components) from vegetables have lower bioavailability than those from animal proteins. Dogs are carnivores—meat eaters. Plant protein is of lower quality than animal protein, relative to optimum canine nutrition.

Fresh drinking water must be available at all times.

Fats

Brittanys must receive adequate amounts of fat in their diets. Fat is a calorie-dense nutrient that contains 9 Kcal (the amount of heat energy required to raise 1 kg of water from 15 to 16°C) per gram. That is more than twice the calories of protein and carbohydrates. This is true of both animal fat and vegetable oil. Preferred taste (palatability) is the principal difference between vegetable oils and animal fats. Both provide adequate fatty acids.

Carbohydrates

Starches, or carbohydrates, are also plant-derived sources of calories. They are important as the principal sources of glucose in human diets, but carbohydrates are not significant in canine nutrition. Dogs don't require carbohydrates, but diets without them are impractical to produce commercially. Dog foods that are high in carbohydrates and contain protein and fat that are also of plant origin are not recommended. The best nutrition for a dog is a food that combines animal protein with plant carbohydrates and fats.

Supplements

When feeding a balanced diet, such as a premium food, no vitamin or mineral supplementation is necessary. Don't feed a bargain brand of dog food and hope to cover its deficiencies with a cheap vitamin-mineral supplement. Check with your veterinarian before feeding any supplements to your Brittany.

In dog foods of the past, protein quality was suspect and amino acid deficiencies were sometimes experienced. At that time, nutritionists recommended adding bone meal and meat, especially liver, to dry dog food diets. Contemporary research by pet food manufacturers, private research foundations, and universities has provided more information about the nutritional needs of our pets. Complete and balanced diets are now available in commercial pet foods.

For those readers who want to read about the intricacies of canine nutrition, purchase a book called *Nutritional Requirements of Dogs, Revised*, from the National Research Council. This book is updated regularly and will answer virtually all of your technical questions about canine nutrition.

Coat supplements are available everywhere and they will rarely endanger your dog's nutritional balance, but are usually unnecessary. Every owner wants their Brittany to be shiny with rich colors, but the best way to attain that appearance is through good nutrition, not from a bottle of coat enhancer. Get a veterinarian's advice before you use lecithin, vitamin A, corn oil, or other coat-enhancing preparations.

Chewsticks and Treats

There are dozens of chew toys in pet supply stores. Rawhide bones, cartilage from pigs ears, cattle hooves, and nylon bones are all good chew toys for Brittanys. Likewise, dog biscuits or treats are available in various forms and sizes. They are harmless unless they are used as a principal source of nutrition. Biscuits and treats do not represent any part of a balanced diet and should be used only when you wish to reward Jill or give her something to do. They are excellent enticements to use when you put her in her crate or leave her in her run for a while.

Soft treats, such as bits of liver or other meat should be reserved for training rewards and shouldn't be fed in large quantities.

Homemade Diets

Diets that are formulated in the family kitchen can often lead to problems. It's best to leave dog food production

These fine Brittanys are in excellent condition.

to those companies that have laboratories, research facilities, and colonies of dogs for feeding trials to prove the value of their products.

Frequency of Feeding

After weaning, each pup should be fed free choice dry food plus two moist meals of mixed canned and dry food daily. The quantity of the moist meals should be gradually increased as the puppy grows. This feeding program should be continued until Jill is six months of age. From six months until she is one year old, the free choice dry food is continued and one moist meal per day is fed. At one year of age, most dogs will do quite nicely on free choice dry food by itself.

The exceptions to this feeding schedule include gluttonous eaters or multiple dog households where other dogs in the home are gluttonous eaters. Another exception is the dog

with a finicky appetite. That condition is rarely seen in Brittanys, but when it occurs, the meals of canned plus dry food may be continued indefinitely. In large breeds that are prone to hip dysplasia and elbow dysplasia, a controlled diet is often necessary to prevent a growth rate that is too rapid.

If free choice feeding isn't a viable option, feed puppies three times daily and dogs that are older than six months twice daily.

Dietary No-No's

Don't feed your Brittany milk of any kind, because it will usually cause diarrhea. Organ meat (liver, heart, or kidney), rich foods, and table scraps may also upset the dog's stomach and interfere with her nutrition. Cooked bones are also a danger to your dog. Chicken or chop bones, steak bones, and some roast bones may splinter when the dog chomps down on them.

Sharp splinters from the bones may lodge in the dog's mouth or throat, or the splinters may be swallowed where they can cause other problems. Ice cream, candy, pizza, potato chips, and a host of other human junk foods are difficult for the dog to digest and should be avoided.

Bad Eating Habits

Fat dogs are often the result of improper feeding habits. If Jill is a gluttonous eater, you must take the responsibility of feeding her meals that won't perpetuate her gluttonous habits and lead to obesity. If she tends toward obesity, measured amounts should be fed, and her weight and condition should be monitored frequently. If she is housed with another dog, it will be necessary to separate them at mealtime. After you have arrived at the maintenance quantity of food to feed, remember to increase it if she is undergoing training or when bird season rolls around.

Adding low-calorie fillers to her diet can also be used to treat obesity in an otherwise healthy dog. Ground carrots, canned green beans, or other low-calorie foods may be added to her balanced diet without upsetting it appreciably.

Older dogs often become lazy and may put on weight. When a dog begins to age and no longer exercises for hours each day, its food must be cut back. A reevaluation of the older dog's nutritional needs should be included in the cutback program, as nutritional requirements change with age. Generally, a higher quality food in less quantity is the answer to old-age canine obesity.

Dogs that seem to gain weight and develop a voracious appetite should be examined. There are a number of health problems, including diabetes that may cause weight gain.

Skinny dogs are often impossible to put weight on. Some Brittanys are so ambitious and energetic that they remain thin all their lives. They burn so many calories in their everyday activities that their bodies can't keep up. It is best to feed such dogs premium foods—free choice, with a meal or two of dry food mixed with canned food each day. If weight loss or decreased energy is seen in an already thin dog, a veterinary examination is needed.

Food and Water Bowls

The best type of bowls are stainless steel. Glass bowls usually don't last long. Fired clay bowls may contain toxins in the paint. Aluminum or plastic bowls are usually porous and may house bacteria. Invest in a pair of heavy stainless steel bowls large enough to hold Jill's feed when she is an adult. Another item to purchase is a rack to keep the bowls upright and to anchor them in place.

If free choice feeding is a part of your dog's nutritional program, fill the feed bowl daily. Don't buy a large self-feeder, or if one is used, be sure to clean it regularly and inspect it frequently for bugs.

Grooming Your Brittany

Factors that Influence Coat Quality

Your Brittany's coat requires more than brushing or combing once in a while. Chip's coat is a reflection of his nutritional status and general condition. If he is maintained on a premium dog food and is exercised often, his coat will probably always look great. Coat supplements are usually an unnecessary expense, but they may be advised under special circumstances.

Internal parasite infestations can also influence the appearance of a dog's coat. Roundworms rob the dog of nutrition, thereby causing dietary insufficiencies. Hookworms cause blood loss and may contribute to coat problems. External parasites such as fleas cause the dog to scratch and also contribute to poor coats.

Pregnancy, whelping, and lactation stress a brood bitch's system and will always cause the bitch to lose coat and have a ratty appearance for several weeks.

A normal dog usually sheds its coat twice a year, and during those times, additional grooming is necessary. As Chip ages, his nutritional needs change, and older dogs often display coat problems in response to their new nutritional needs.

Coat care is a major consideration for dog owners, and even if your Brittany's coat is shiny and has a natural sheen, you aren't relieved of your grooming responsibilities. Brushing, combing, and occasional bathing is a necessary part of dog ownership. Routine grooming procedures should be scheduled and not left to "when I find time." An equally bad plan is to delegate the dog's grooming duties to an unsupervised youngster.

When to Groom

Grooming your Brittany pup is an important part of his bonding and training and should begin shortly after you acquire the pup. The time you spend grooming Chip will establish trust and obedience, and if your schedule allows, it may become a part of his daily experience. The procedure is beneficial from a training standpoint because the puppy is taught to stand or sit still on the table while you groom him. Daily examination of Chip's pads accustoms him to handling, and he is less likely to resist having his feet touched as he matures.

If you hold the dog on your lap when grooming him, it will encourage him to chew, try to play, or escape. Instead, put him on a towel that is draped across a table or countertop and is held in place by picnic table clips. Grooming is serious business; don't let Chip jump from the table while you're combing him. Be sure he understands the necessity and certainty of the procedure. Educational discipline isn't the only reason to take a positive attitude about grooming. Remember that a pup bonds to the person with whom he spends the most time. He respects the person who handles him the most; you are establishing yourself as his leader.

After Chip has outgrown puppyhood, if he is exercised in the country or is performing as a hunting dog, grooming should be a routine procedure that follows every run in the field. You can find and remove thistles and cheat-grass awns from between his toes and those that are tangled in his ear hair. Minor

Busy Brittanys require regular grooming.

When this pup gets his bird delivered, he'll need grooming.

footpad injuries can be medicated as well as eye irritations that result from running in dense cover and brush.

While grooming, you may discover minor health problems, such as an early ear infection, fleas, or ticks. When these problems are recognized early, the treatment is far less extensive and less costly than if allowed to progress.

Grooming may be a chore in the beginning; many pups refuse to stand still. Sometimes they fidget, nip, and wriggle and the routine may be exasperating to a new dog owner. Have patience, stay with it, and the results will warrant the struggle!

Calluses

Routine grooming includes being alert for abnormalities that may be present on the skin, as well as on the coat. Older dogs often develop skin tumors, and hunting dogs occasionally suffer scratches and abrasions. Calluses are rarely a problem in pet Brit-

tanys but they are common in kenneled dogs that are kept on concrete or wooden floors. They are unsightly, but they aren't generally a serious health problem unless they become infected. Callus formation usually begins on the outside of the dogs' elbows and later they may form on the hocks, sides of the feet, and on the hipbones. If the calluses are hard, cracked, and infected, consult your veterinarian.

Routine care for dogs that are kept on hard surfaces should include lanolin and vitamin E applications to callus formations to keep them soft and pliable. Calluses may be of considerable concern in your Brittany after the age of six or seven.

Tooth Care

Dental considerations are a part of the grooming of your pet. You should make a habit of brushing your Brittany's teeth weekly from the time he is a puppy. Between three and six months of age, Chip may have two sets of teeth. It's not uncommon for a dog's permanent teeth to emerge from the gums before the deciduous (temporary) teeth are lost. If the baby teeth are loose and wriggly, no treatment is necessary. If the permanent teeth have reached full growth and the baby teeth are still anchored solidly in the gums, those deciduous teeth might require extraction. Don't attempt this at home. A pair of pliers will only break the teeth off, make Chip mad, and you will still have the expense of a trip to the animal hospital.

If the baby teeth are not removed when they are solidly situated beside the permanent teeth, they may interfere with the normal alignment of the adult teeth. Even if that is not the case, the tight space between the two sets of teeth may collect hair and debris and contribute to halitosis and gum infection (gingivitis).

If your dog is given rawhide or nylon bones to chew and is fed primarily dry dog food, his teeth shouldn't require much routine care. Dogs rarely develop cavities unless the teeth are broken. Older dogs and dogs that don't chew a lot may be subject to dental tartar deposits if their teeth aren't brushed regularly. As the tartar accumulates, it invades and erodes the gums and causes bacterial infections to begin. If allowed to progress unchecked, this gingivitis will eventually cause the teeth to loosen. Chronic gum infection may predispose older dogs to arthritis and heart and kidney disease.

Dental plaque can be prevented if you routinely brush Chip's teeth every time you groom him. If soft yellow tartar is seen, try cleaning the teeth with gauze pads moistened with hydrogen peroxide. The peroxide will help control gingivitis, and often will dissolve the soft, early dental tartar. Canine toothpaste and toothbrushes are available from your veterinarian or from pet supply stores. Most adult dogs don't

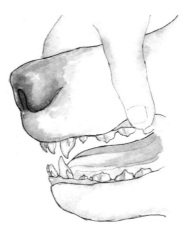

A double set of teeth sometimes causes a problem.

enjoy having their teeth brushed, but if you begin when he is still a puppy, Chip will become accustomed to it and accept this oral hygiene process. If tartar accumulates despite your efforts, your veterinarian can scale the teeth with ultrasonic equipment and dental instruments. Sometimes that procedure requires a short-acting general anesthetic.

Brush your Brittany's teeth weekly.

HOW-TO:
Groom
Your Brittany

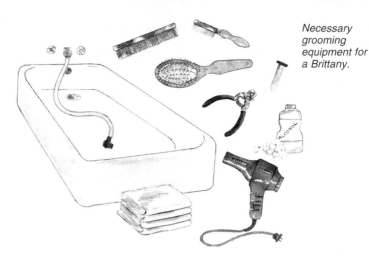

Necessary grooming equipment for a Brittany.

Only bathe Chip if his coat is deeply soiled, fouled, or shortly before a dog show. When Chip runs afoul of a skunk or finds something particularly rancid to roll in along the hiking trail, it is usually time for a bath. A bath will also help finalize the semi-annual seasonal shedding. Pick a warm day or plan to spend half an hour in the house with your Brittany. Have available the following equipment.

• Stainless steel comb with wide-set teeth
• Flea comb
• Pin brush with short, wire bristles
• Scissors-type nail trimmer
• Styptic shaving stick
• Electric hair dryer with warm setting
• Bathtub (with hair-collecting drain stopper)
• Sprayer hose connected to a faucet
• Mild dog shampoo without insecticides
• Stack of dry towels.

Great care and sharp nail trimmers are a must.

• Cotton balls
• Rubbing alcohol

Combing

Take your time when combing and brushing all of the loose hair from Chip's coat. Combing helps to get the dead hair off the dog and into the brush instead of on the furniture and carpet. Don't forget to reward Chip when he stands quietly, and don't be too cross if he is impatient and anxious for you to finish. When combing his coat, pay particular attention to the pelvic area, immediately in front of his tail. After the initial combing and brushing, run the fine-tooth flea comb through the hair of this area. If fleas are present, they will hop out ahead of the comb or will be caught in the teeth of the comb.

Nails

Trim Chip's nails, using a sharp nail trimmer of the scissors type. Never use a dull instrument. Long, pointed puppy nails often need attention weekly. For active outdoor, adult Brittanys,

the nails of the forefeet require trimming only when they are heard pecking on the tile floor. Hind nails suffer less wear than the front ones, since they aren't used in digging; they often need your attention on a regular basis. Old dogs' nails should be checked more often than younger animals.

Nail trimming is not difficult, but in the beginning, it sometimes requires two sets of hands and a firm conviction on the owner's part. If this routine is begun when Chip is a puppy, it will be better accepted all his life.

Most Brittany's nails are light in color, and at least a few are sufficiently transparent to see the blood vessels forming a point in the core of the nail. Your first cut should be just beyond that forward-pointing, V-shaped vascular structure. By visually measuring the length of the white nail after trimming it, you should have a good idea about how much to take off the darker nails.

If in doubt, starting at the tip, begin cutting off thin serial slices of the nail. As you progress, you will discover that the nail becomes softer with each slice. Near the tip of the nails, the cross-sections of the slices will be hollow at the bottom, an inverted V-shape. As you near the blood vessels, the slices will become more nearly circular when viewed in cross-sections.

A Dremel Moto-Tool® that is equipped with a sandpaper drum can also be used to shorten and sand off rough edges from toenails. They grind very quickly, and you must be careful when using this high-speed tool.

Slight bleeding from a nail shouldn't be cause for alarm. The bleeding isn't likely to be profuse, but it may be persistent. A few drops of blood always look like a quart when spread over a white tile floor. To stop the bleeding, press a dampened styptic shaving-stick firmly to the bleeding nail, hold it in place for several minutes and keep the dog confined to his crate for an hour after stopping the bleeding.

Ears

An examination of Chip's ears should follow each trip to the field, whether hunting or just walking in the woods. Ear cleaning is an important part of regular grooming in hunting dogs. If you notice a significant amount of wax or dirt in the outer ear canal, it is easily cleaned with a cotton ball that has been moistened with alcohol. Never pour any cleaning solution into Chip's ears unless advised to do so by your veterinarian. When you are combing and inspecting Chip's ears, be aware of unusual sensitivity. If

he scratches at either or both ears, or holds his head tipped to the side when you touch one, have the ears examined before initiating any treatment. Grass-awns are commonly found in the outer ear canals of field dogs and may lead to serious infections. (See Health Care chapter on page 71.)

Eyes

Inspect Chip's eyes each time he runs in the field, as well as when he is groomed. Look for redness, irritation, and foreign material. It is fairly common for field dogs to collect grass seeds or minute plant particles under one of their eyelids. A grass seed that is trapped under an eyelid will cause the dog to squint and may require a visit to the veterinarian. It will be easier (and cheaper) to remove the foreign material before it has rubbed on the cornea and created a corneal ulcer that must also be treated.

Bathing

When bathing is deemed necessary, place Chip in the bathtub and soak his coat thoroughly with warm water, using the spray nozzle that is held close to his skin. Using a mild human shampoo sparingly, work it into a good lather. Keep the soap well away from his face and eyes, and don't squirt water into his ears. When satisfied that the entire coat has been lathered, hold the spray nozzle close to his skin and work it around to rinse the soap from his coat, going over his body several times, until all of the shampoo is gone.

Hold the spray close to the skin.

Towel Chip several times, rubbing his coat vigorously and changing towels frequently, to squeeze as much water as possible from the coat. Take him out of the bathtub and using the warm setting on the dryer, complete the drying procedure. This last part of the program is sometimes unnecessary during warm summer days.

Squeeze most of the water from the coat with towels.

Work for Your Brittany

Multipurpose Dog

Several AKC breeds are called "dual-purpose" dogs to indicate that individuals of that breed participate in conformation shows as well as in field trial competition. Dual purpose is a term that has found true meaning in the versatile Brittany. This breed is making more and more appearances in the show ring and is routinely achieving recognition in other arenas as well.

The intelligent and biddable Brittany often does well in obedience trials; with some training Brittanys excel in field trials, and many serve the weekend sportsman's hunting needs as well. Willingness and adaptability enhance the Brittanys' talents. Their scenting capabilities serve them well in AKC tracking trials. Likewise, their responsiveness to trainers' commands and their fun loving energy makes them good candidates for agility trials.

The size and ease of care of Brittanys makes them ideal companion dogs, yard dogs, and children's playmates. Many well-mannered Brittanys sleep at the foot of their owners' beds at night. To achieve an AKC Canine Good Citizen (CGC) award is usually a simple task for the easily handled Brittany.

Hunting and Retrieving

Many Brittanys are purchased with no intention of field competition, but rather for private weekend shooting expeditions. They help their owners put grouse, quail, pheasants, and other game birds on the table for Sunday dinner.

Training Jill to hunt should be no problem. The breed has been kept as a gun dog for many years; pointing and retrieving are natural to most Brittanys. Many trainers introduce puppies to feathered dummies at a very young age (perhaps five or six weeks), then discontinue training until a time when the dog's mental maturity indicates that its attention span can handle more intense training.

An anecdote will help illustrate how intelligent this dog is and how it is always thinking, despite what it has been taught.

"Duke" accompanied her trainer and a greenhorn hunter to the field. The gentleman had never before hunted over a dog and didn't know what to expect. The trainer went from the field to move his truck and returned to find Duke on point to the left of the hunter. The hunter, unsure of what he was about, ignored Duke's point, flushed and shot a quail as it broke cover on his right. Duke continued to stand on his original point for a short while, then he ran to retrieve the quail for the hunter, returned, and resumed his point on the original find. Duke proved that his instinct and training were both in tune that day!

Knowledge and patience are the two key attributes of a gun dog trainer. Like other disciplines, training a hunting dog requires regular practice sessions. There is no right or wrong way to train a dog in any discipline, and the method of training will depend on the instructor's experience and knowledge. For the average weekend hunter, training your own dog can be fun and rewarding.

Formal retriever training, field trial training, and gun dog training are

Retrieving waterfowl is taken in stride.

beyond the scope of this manual but some hints are offered to help you start the pup. Assuming that Jill has inherited the Brittany's natural pointing and retrieving tendencies, the process is quite simple. You may start training her when she is very young. If she doesn't catch on quickly, wait a week before you try it again. Don't repeat any exercises so frequently that she loses interest in them.

A word of caution: If you aren't sure what you are doing, get help. Obtain advice from an experienced gun dog trainer, buy a book and follow directions, join a club, but don't, under any circumstances, take a chance of spoiling a fine Brittany because of your own lack of knowledge.

To minimize confusion and establish consistency, training should be performed by one instructor, if possible. This is doubly important in the case of a family dog, where one member of the family typically plays with the dog and another is responsible for discipline or training. Simple obedience commands must be mastered before the dog can begin gun training.

Dummies

Use a canvas or feathered dummy, a softball, or a fabric-covered lightweight object, such as a tennis ball tied into a sock. These objects are soft to the dog's mouth and will serve you best when teaching your Brittany to fetch.

Hard or heavy objects such as sticks, bones, hard rubber balls, or golf balls should never be used when training a hunting dog. They will encourage Jill to bite down hard and will promote the development of a "hard mouth" in your Brittany. You can increase her enthusiasm for fetching by adding a couple of drops of scent on the

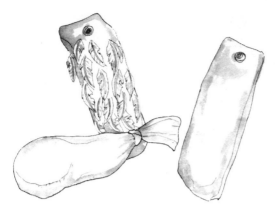

Dummies for teaching your Brittany pup to retrieve should be soft.

dummy being used. Bird scents are available at sporting goods stores, or in a pinch, you can rub a hotdog on the dummy.

In the beginning it is important to give Jill a reward after each successful retrieve. This reinforces the instinctive retriever action of the dog and elicits better cooperation when she is taken to the field. After a few sessions, a pat on the head and a *"Good dog"* takes the place of the reward.

Start your retriever's education in the backyard. After attaching a long, lightweight nylon cord to her collar, get Jill's attention by waving the dummy closely in front of her nose. Then toss the dummy a short distance in front of her, accompanying the toss with the command *"Jill, fetch."* When she has responded and picked up the dummy, call her, as you gently coax her to return to you. When she reaches you, tell her *"Give,"* or *"Out,"* and take the dummy from her mouth. Don't allow her to drop it. If she refuses to part with the dummy on command, offer her a tidbit; she can't accept it without handing you the dummy. Don't forcibly pull the dummy from her, this is no time to

play tug-of-war! After she give you the dummy, praise her for a job well done and then repeat the exercise. It is important that you repeat this fetching exercise daily, but not for extended periods of time. Don't allow the dog to become bored with the game. Fetching can sometimes be integrated into her other training sessions when she is taught to *come, sit, stay, whoa,* and other obedience commands.

Scent

A variation of the dummy training tends to stimulate a birdy Brittany's interest. Obtain a scented game bird wing and hide it in the tall grass. (A pigeon or dove wing with a couple of drops of scent is fine.) Let Jill discover it on her own when she is on the long nylon check cord. When she stops to savor the odor of the wing for a second, steady the pup with slight pressure on the cord, and quietly tell her *"Whoa."* Your voice and action will let her know that this is an important smell to remember. A scented bird wing will keep best in a plastic bag in your freezer when not in use.

Flash Point

Take Jill to a nearby field or meadow where birds abound. They need not be game birds in the beginning. You will probably see the pup periodically assume an instinctive pointing stance for a split second when she perceives the presence of birds under cover. This pause is called a flash point and is to be encouraged. When you have recognized the flash point repeatedly, it is time to teach her to hold the point.

Quietly tell Jill *"Whoa,"* as you move to her side while she assumes the pointing stance. Then with gentle hands and voice encourage her to remain steady on point. You can then accompany her to flush the birds. The *whoa* command is very important for a field dog to master. If she always pauses when she hears *whoa*, your voice intonations can change to make her hold the flash point or to stop suddenly in her tracks.

Place a scented bird wing on the end of a fishing line and hide it in the grass. When she has stopped and has held her flash point for a second, hold her gently with the nylon check line and with your fishing pole release the bird wing by jerking it in the air. Tell Jill *"Whoa"* to teach her to stand still when birds fly away. This command will also teach her not to chase birds that land and fly away in your yard. A well-trained dog will point birds, not chase them.

Teaching the pup to hold the flash point.

Guns

A cap pistol or .22-caliber gun loaded with blanks is often used in early gun dog training. Later, after the dog has become accustomed to the noise, a shotgun can be used. The object is to correlate the noise of the gun with fetching the dummy. Always fire the gun in front of the dog so that the concussion and noise will be directed away from her. Never fire a gun so close to the dog's head as to cause hearing impairment. Their sense of hearing is extremely sensitive and must be protected at all costs.

Jill should quickly become accustomed to the sound of a gun being fired in her immediate proximity. She should soon master backyard fetching, and her instinct to point birds under cover will become as natural as her name.

At this time, Jill is probably ready for her first expedition into the field. Be patient. Don't expect miracles. In the beginning, keep a long checkline on Jill's collar to hold her in. Don't allow her to develop the bad habit of hesitating on point for a second, then rushing in to flush the birds before you are ready. Talk to her; teach her to listen to your voice and instructions. When

she does hold a point and gives you time to reach her, pet her and praise her. Then move in to flush, shoot, and send her to fetch. If Jill points a robin or sparrow that's OK, her scent discrimination will develop in time.

This is only a brief discussion of gun dog training. Many books have been written on this subject. This discussion was only intended to let you know about some of the basic steps to be taken. If you hunt her regularly, you probably will want Jill professionally trained, or you will join a hunting club and take advantage of the instruction that is offered. If you are a seasonal, weekend hunter, you can probably train your Brittany yourself, but don't hesitate to confer with friends and professionals in the local Brittany club.

Field Trials

English bird-dog competition has been active since 1865, and field trials have been held in the United States since 1874. They are intended to prove the value of dogs in the performance of the duties for which they were bred. Like herding trials, retriever trials, tracking trials, and other similar competitions, bird-dog competitions

Pointing is natural for Brittanys.

after World War II when the trials became more specialized and competition got tougher. Professional handlers and trainers took their places beside the dogs instead of owners and weekend shooters.

The first Brittany to win a field trial in the United States was in 1935 when "Frache du Cosquerou" earned third place in a trial in New Jersey. Brittanys were originally at a definite disadvantage because trial judges were accustomed to judging dogs with long, feathered tails. Although Brittanys excelled as bird finders, they were routinely marked low in the "class" category.

In 1942 the American Brittany Club formed and took charge of the all-Brittany field trials. In 1943, the AKC licensed its first Brittany field trial. The first AKC Field Champion and the first Dual Champion Brittany was *Brit of Bellows Falls*, who won those honors in 1946.

Field Champion

To be awarded a Field Champion title, a dog must win ten points in judged trials. Points are awarded to the first place winner in a regular stake competition. In the 1980s there were about 5,000 Brittanys that participated in field trials. The competition among top Brittanys produced about 700 Field Champions, and about one in five of these Field Champions possessed the coveted title of "dual champion." A dual champion is a dog that has been awarded the title of Champion of Record in AKC conformation shows, plus a Field Champion title in field trials. There were 240 dual champion Brittanys reported in the 1985 *Book of the Brittany* and 405 as of October 1995.

Brittany Nationals

The American Brittany Club also sponsors the Brittany Nationals. This

test dogs of similar heritage against one another in field performance. Field trial competition was very likely established to furnish bird-dog owners a way to compare their dogs; the trials established bragging rights for the owner of today's "best dog."

Hunting dog owners long ago recognized the importance of competition under a set of rules that was equal for all dogs and handlers. After all, how can you say that your dog is a better hunting dog than mine is unless the same rules are followed and trained judges are on hand to make the final decisions? With standardized scoring, there is still some degree of interpretation that must be made by the judges, but by applying set rules to certain activities, the best dog usually will win the competition.

Early American field trials were open only to pointers and setters and were a way to prove which bench show dogs of those breeds should be bred. A field trial was the only reliable way of separating the true working dogs from the frill and fluff that were thought to dominate bench shows. Field trial dogs came into their own is field trial competition of the finest order with the best Brittanys in America vying for the AKC title "National Champion." This event has nationwide representation and is the ultimate Brittany competition in the United States.

Specialty field trials are open to all Brittanys. Each year the American Brittany Club sponsors a Pheasant Classic, Quail Classic, Prairie Chicken Classic, Grouse Classic, Gun Dog Classic, and Chukar Classic.

Field Trial Classes

Official AKC field trial classes are: Open Puppy, Open Derby, Gun Dog Stake, All-Age Stake, Limited Gun Dog Stake, and Limited All-Age Stake. They are separated by the dogs' ages and prior wins.

Amateur field trials attract many novices in the sport; if you want to receive more information about these trials, contact the Amateur Field Trial Clubs of America whose address is listed in the back of this book. For more information and Brittany field trial data, see Rheta Cartmell's *Book of the American Brittany*, published by the American Brittany Club and available from that organization (their address is provided in the back of this book). Regional and local Brittany clubs will furnish information regarding getting started in field trial competition.

Hunting Tests

The AKC hunting test program for pointers was begun in 1985. This "true" testing program complements the formal field trials. The tests of this program give owners another way to evaluate their bird dogs against written hunting standards without competition as well as an informal and fun way to exhibit their dogs. The tests are judged by professionals and are meant to identify dogs that possess superior hunting abilities. Awards are made according to performance in the

Training a Brittany for water retrieving is easy.

field under simulated, nearly natural hunting conditions. Winners are awarded the AKC suffix titles of Junior Hunter (JH), Senior Hunter (SH), and Master Hunter (MH), which are added to the dogs registered names.

Field trials simulate actual hunting conditions

Obedience Trials

AKC Obedience Trials are competitions for registered dogs that aren't limited to dogs of similar heritage; a Brittany may be entered in competition with dozens of dogs of many different breeds. As in other AKC events, obedience clubs must first meet strict club standards and be licensed by the AKC to hold an obedience trial.

An obedience trial is a sport that demonstrates the usefulness of the purebred dog as a companion. It involves more than the dog's ability to follow a routine and perform certain tasks. The dogs in each of the various classes perform the same exercises in the same way in order to be compared and scored by the judges. They are awarded points as they are scored according to their performances. The primary objective of obedience trials is to prove the training and conditioning of dogs in every conceivable circumstance. The purpose of obedience trials is to promote exemplary dog behavior in all situations in public places and in the presence of other dogs and handlers.

Well-trained Brittanys love to show off in obedience trials.

This sport judges not only the training of dogs but also their enjoyment and willingness to perform the work. In that regard, obedience trials are very similar to field trials. The dogs must certainly be properly trained, but to do well, they must also show a certain "flare" or "class" in accomplishing the different tests. Likewise, the dogs must be practiced and smooth, but the judges also look for happy dogs, not robots.

Rules

There are many rules promulgated for the conduct and appearance of obedience dogs. For instance, dogs that have had plastic surgery to correct a congenital defect may participate in obedience trials, provided that the dogs have also been neutered. In other words, obedience trials are not beauty contests. Spaying, neutering, or coat defects do not eliminate dogs from participation in obedience trials. However, lame or bandaged dogs may not compete and neither can dogs that have been dyed or artificially colored.

If a handler can't control her dog, if she interferes with a competitor, or abuses her dog, she will be excused from competition. Handicapped handlers may compete in obedience trials, and the judge will usually modify the rules to permit disabled handlers to participate. Their dogs are required to perform all the usual exercises, but the rules allow handicapped persons to enter and exhibit their dogs.

Classes, Exercises, and Awards

Novice A classes and Novice B classes are for dogs of six months or older that haven't won a Companion Dog (CD) title. Novice exercises consist of heel on leash and figure eight; stand for examination; heel free; recall; long sit; and long down.

The AKC awards a CD title certificate to a dog that has received qualifying scores at three licensed or member obedience trials, under three different judges, provided that at least six dogs were competing in each trial.

Open A class is for dogs that have won the CD title but haven't won a Companion Dog Excellent (CDX) title. The dog's owner or a member of her family must handle the dog.

Open B class is for dogs that have won the CD title or a CDX title or a Utility Dog (UD) title. The owner or any other person may handle these dogs.

The exercises for open classes consist of heel free and figure eight; drop on recall; retrieve on flat; retrieve over high jump; broad jump; long sit; and long down.

A CDX title may be awarded by the AKC to a dog that has received qualifying scores at three obedience trials judged by three different judges.

Utility A class is for dogs that have won the CDX title but not the UD title. The dog's owner or member of her immediate family must handle them.

Utility B class is for dogs that have won the CDX or UD title, and any person may handle them.

Utility exercises involve a signal exercise; scent discrimination article 1; scent discrimination article 2; directed retrieve; moving stand and examination; and directed jumping.

A UD title is awarded to a dog that has received qualifying scores by three different judges in three obedience trials. There were 55 Brittany UDs reported in the 1985 *Book of the Brittany*, and four or five new Brittanys earn this title every year.

Utility dogs may earn points toward the coveted Obedience Trial Champion (OTCh) title. These points are awarded for each first or second place ribbon won in UD classes, according to the number of dogs competing. A dog must accumulate no less than 100 points under specific circumstances.

A Triple Champion is a dog that has earned a Field Champion title, a Champion of Record title, and an Obedience Trial Championship title.

Tracking Dog

Brittanys are also eligible to compete in tracking tests. This is another sport in which Jill's excellent scent abilities should keep her in good stead. Dogs are judged on their ability to follow a track that was plotted and laid out in the absence of all dogs and handlers.

The articles that are used to establish a scent track are about the size of a glove or wallet. A person who is a stranger to the participating dog lays the track out following the outline that has been plotted by a judge. The articles are dropped on the track by the "track layer," and they can't be visible for more than 20 feet nor can they be covered with anything that might conceal them.

Long leashes are used on the tracking dog harnesses, and the handler follows the dog at a distance of no less than 20 feet. Handlers may give verbal commands and encouragement to the dog, but can't indicate the location or direction of the track. There is no time limit on the track but if Jill stops working the trail, she is marked failed.

Levels and Awards

There are several levels of tracking tests. Tracking Test/TD is for dogs more than six months old who haven't earned a TD, TDX, or VST title. The Tracking Dog (TD) title is earned when a registered dog is certified by two judges to have passed a licensed or member-club Tracking Test/TD.

A Tracking Test/TDX is available to dogs that have already earned a TD title. The Tracking Dog Excellent (TDX) title is awarded to dogs that have been certified by two judges to have passed two Tracking Test/TDX.

Happy companion dogs make good agility dogs.

The length of track and the complexity of the turns and other items to increase the difficulty of trails are increased in the TDX tracks; even more complexities are included in the Tracking Test/VST.

Variable Surface Tracking (VST) verifies the dog's ability to recognize

In tracking tests, the handler can give the dog encouragement, but no directions.

and follow human scent while adapting to changing scenting conditions. Each track has a minimum of three different surfaces, including vegetation and two areas devoid of vegetation such as concrete, asphalt, gravel, sand, hard pan, or mulch. No obstacles are used in this test, but tracks may be laid out through buildings, breezeways, shelters, and open garages.

Four articles are used in the VST test—each of which is different from the others and all of which may be easily picked up by the dog. The articles are made of leather, plastic, metal, and fabric.

Tracking is a sport, and dogs that excel do so because they have highly sensitive noses and enjoy using them. Tracking isn't competitive in the same sense that other work is. There is a camaraderie among handlers, win or lose, and it is a pleasurable event to attend as a spectator. Contact the AKC for further information about tracking tests.

Agility Trials

Agility tests demonstrate training, willingness, and energy of dogs as they work with their handlers. There are several levels of serious competition, but all in all, agility trials are fun events. AKC agility trials are open to any AKC registered dog, and as in other AKC events (except conformation shows or field trials), no restrictions are placed on participation by neutered dogs.

The youngest age that a dog may participate is 12 months, and there are divisions and classes to cover handlers and dogs at every stage of training. The titles earned are Novice Agility (NA), Open Agility (OA), Agility Excellent (AX), and Master Agility Excellent (MX).

Titles and Awards

In order for a dog to earn the titles NA, OA, and AX, it must acquire qualifying scores in three separate trials under two different judges. One title must be earned before the next level of competition is attempted. The MX title is earned after a dog has been awarded the AX title and receives qualifying scores in ten separate trials.

This Brittany is getting plenty of exercise.

Obstacles

Agility trials use many props and obstacles that are sized according to the size of the dog. Obstacles include broad and high jumps, an A-frame to climb over, an elevated dog walk to traverse, a teetering seesaw to master, a table to pause on, an open tunnel to go through, a closed tunnel made of fabric that the dog must push its way through, a set of poles to weave, and

Agility trials are fun for dogs and for their handlers.

double bar jumps. There is also a window that the dog must jump through and an identified area of the ground where the competitor must pause.

Agility obstacles are laid out in a course, and the handler runs along beside, behind, or in front of the dog that is performing. Handlers may not touch the dog at any time. The scoring is based on the course distance and is timed. A time penalty is awarded for minor infractions, and a refusal to try an obstacle penalizes the participating dog five points. Refusals are not permitted for dogs that are competing in the AX class.

Agility trials have been popular in Europe for many years and have been catching on very well in the United States recently. They are fun for spectators and contestants alike, and if you have an active agility club in your area, attend a trial. A word of warning: They are contagious. The participants seem to be having great fun, yet the training that both dogs and handlers undergo is extensive. If you have a Brittany of any age that is biddable and loves to please, agility work may be for you.

Good Citizen Certificate

Dog clubs throughout the United States administer Canine Good Citizen (CGC) tests for dogs. The AKC sponsors this program, which is designed to promote good manners and behavior. Owners have their dogs evaluated for ten different activities that help to assure that their dogs are good neighbors. No points are involved; the scoring is a simple pass or fail evaluation. The essential, easily taught activities include allowing a stranger to approach, walking naturally on a loose lead, walking through a crowd, sitting for examination, reacting to a strange dog, and reacting to a distraction such as a door suddenly closing or a jogger running by.

AKC member clubs make good citizen evaluations, and information about them may be obtained by contacting the AKC or an all-breed club in your community. Having a CGC certificate hanging on your wall is evidence that your Brittany has been trained. It also means that you love your dog enough to spend the time training it and that Jill is a good neighbor.

Health Care

Choosing a Good Veterinarian

Nothing will enhance your enjoyment of owning a Brittany more than a good relationship with an understanding veterinarian. An animal health professional who cares about your pet and prescribes a sound preventive healthcare program is an asset to dog owners. He or she will have advice about the initial selection of a dog, information regarding routine and specialized care, and an active, aggressive treatment plan for an injured or ill patient that needs medical or surgical care. The veterinarian is a resource that you can ill afford to be without. The question is: How do you choose a "good" veterinarian?

Don't be afraid to "shop." Arrange an appointment with a local veterinarian before you buy your Brittany. A reliable, concerned professional will give you a few minutes of her or his time and will welcome your visit and your inquiries. Ask how out-of-hours emergencies are handled. If off-hours treatment is not provided and such calls are referred to an emergency care clinic, check it out as well. Arrange for a tour of the animal hospital at a convenient time. Check the available facilities and equipment, for cleanliness and organization. See if the doctor and staff appear friendly, caring, knowledgeable, and are ready to share their knowledge with you. Explain your animal healthcare needs, and see how the veterinarian responds to them.

Communicating With a Veterinarian

Communication is the key to a good relationship with your veterinarian.

Look for a veterinarian who is open and willing to listen to you. Try to find one who will spend time explaining procedures and one who isn't too busy to tell you why a recommendation is being made. Although professional fees alone are poor criteria for selecting a veterinarian, check on the cost of spaying your female or neutering your male Brittany. Obtain a fee schedule or inquire about the fees that are charged for routine examinations, vaccinations, fecal exams, and worm treatment. Ask about heartworm, flea, and tick preventive plans and their cost.

Make notes. A good veterinarian won't mind if you take notes. It is important to let the professional know that you are placing your trust in her or him and that you don't take this relationship lightly. The professional should realize that he or she is sharing the stewardship of a pet with you; you are on the same team. If the veterinarian resists being interviewed, look for another. If the professional doesn't share your concern about reliable, effective preventive care, you are in the wrong hospital. If she or he has no time for you as a prospective dog owner and client, how much more time will he or she have for your pet?

After you have acquired your Brittany, check out the veterinarian's tableside manners. How does she or he handle pets? Is he or she in such a hurry that there is no time for small talk and a quick rub of a puppy's chin? Does he seem comfortable with your pet?

If you weren't present at your puppy's prepurchase examination, call the examining veterinarian and talk with

Timely vaccinations will protect a Brittany from most diseases.

Preventive medicine keeps this Brittany in good hunting condition.

him or her. Better yet, take Chip to your own veterinarian for another evaluation. Present the health documents that came with the pup and ask questions about Chip's future vaccination requirements. Be sure to jot down the recommendations offered. Obtain advice about specific parasite control, including internal, external, and blood parasites. Ask about Lyme disease, valley fever, or other exotic diseases that may be endemic in your area.

This early appointment with your veterinarian is an excellent time to discuss spaying or neutering. If you anticipate boarding Chip at any time, ask for kennel referrals. If you aren't sure you can clip your pet's nails, ask the professional to teach you.

Dealing With Emergencies and Illnesses

If your Brittany is ill—regardless of whether his illness is discovered in the field or in his kennel—there are certain steps to take prior to calling the veterinarian.

Poisoning

If you have reason to believe that Chip has been poisoned and the causative agent is not available, get him to a veterinarian immediately. If you have found some of the poisonous agent or a label from the bottle or can, take it with you. If the label instructs you to induce vomiting, you can do so by placing about a teaspoonful of salt on the back of the dog's tongue. A tablespoon of hydrogen peroxide given orally will also induce vomiting.

Car Accidents

These emergencies are seen occasionally in hunting situations and when the dog runs free at home. They usually require professional help. First, control any visible bleeding and keep the dog quiet and warm. Use a jacket or blanket as a stretcher and transport Chip to the veterinarian immediately. Always muzzle the dog before you handle him.

Convulsions

If the dog has no history of epilepsy, try to ascertain the cause of his seizure. It may be the result of a head injury or poisoning. In any case, try to prevent Chip from injuring himself; wrap him in a blanket or coat and waste no time getting him to the veterinary hospital. (See discussion of epilepsy on page 83.)

Home Evaluation of a Sick Brittany

Your dog first-aid kit should contain a thermometer. If Chip appears to be ill, take his rectal temperature. The normal range is from 101.5 to 102.5°F (38.5–39.5°C). Look at the color of the membranes of his mouth; normally they are bright pink, if they are dark or pale he could be in serious trouble. Check his breathing; is his respiration panting or is it shallow or labored? Take his pulse; a dog's normal heart rate is between 70 and 90 beats per minute. The pulse can be taken by pressing your finger against the inside of his thigh, about midway between his stifle (knee) and hip. Look at his eyes; are they bright or are they red and inflamed, dull, or discharging pus? Has he been coughing or sneezing? When did he eat last? Have you seen his stool lately, and if so, was it normal? Has he vomited in the recent past, and if so, was the vomitus bloody, mucoid, or filled with foreign material?

After you have recorded your findings, call your veterinarian for advice or for an appointment. Your veterinarian will appreciate your thoroughness and will be better able to help you. Remember that communication with your healthcare professional is a two-

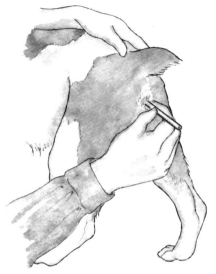

An elevated temperature is one of the first indicators of illness.

way street. Don't wait a day or two to see if the dog gets better unless you are advised to do so.

Happy, healthy Brittany puppies, entertaining each other.

73

HOW-TO:
Treat Emergencies

Emergencies take many forms. Those circumstances that are life threatening are rarely encountered in dogs that are confined to the backyard but when the security of a fenced yard is left behind, more emergency situations may be met.

Fortunately, many of our cars and hunting vehicles are equipped with cellular phones today. When an emergency occurs, contact your veterinarian immediately, ask her or his advice, and let him or her know that you're on your way, and estimate the time you expect to arrive at the hospital.

Always carry a first-aid kit when you are out for an afternoon with your dog. The kit

Pressure bandages are used to stop bleeding.

should include bandages, hydrogen peroxide, a tourniquet, eyewash, tape, and several rolls of gauze. A 4-foot piece of soft cotton cord such as a venetian-blind cord makes a great muzzle and should be included in your first-aid kit.

Muzzle

The mildest mannered dog will often snap or bite viciously when he is injured and feels threatened. Before you handle any injured dog, take the precaution to muzzle him. Approach Chip slowly, lower yourself to his level, and speak to him in a soft voice. Then, tie a single loose knot in the center of the length of cord and slip the loop over Chip's muzzle. Pull the knot snugly on top of his muzzle and then tie the ends of the cord beneath his muzzle with another single knot. Then take the ends of the cord behind his ears and tie the ends together again with a double knot. The muzzle is now snugly in place. If you don't have a muzzle cord in your first-

Muzzling the dog before he is handled is a necessary precaution for a badly hurt dog.

aid kit, tear a 4-foot piece of gauze from a bandage roll and substitute it for the cord.

If Chip is bleeding, find its source and evaluate the amount of blood that is being lost. Keep him quiet. Obtain a blanket or take your jacket to serve as a stretcher for the injured dog. It is important to handle the dog minimally to prevent further damage.

Barbed Wire Cuts

Sometimes a hard-running dog will encounter barbed wire that has been torn from a fence and lies hidden in the weeds. The lacerations that result may be nothing more than minor scratches or skin tears that can wait a few hours for treatment. However, barbed wire is capable of inflicting more serious wounds and may nearly amputate a leg. When any laceration or puncture wound is inflicted, examine the dog carefully to determine how serious the wound is. If the skin tear is significant (more than 1-inch long), put a leash on the dog and call a halt to the hunting.

If the laceration is large, and particularly if it extends deeply into the muscle, either hold Chip still and bring your car to him or pick him up and carry him to the car. Don't let him run back to the car because this will further contaminate the wound with tiny weed seeds and other debris that will be difficult to wash from the wound.

If the wound is bleeding, a pressure bandage should be placed directly over the wound to control the hemorrhage. If a bandage can't be placed on the wound, control the bleeding with finger pressure. Don't use a tourniquet unless there is no other way to stop the bleeding. If a tourniquet is needed, it can be formed from a bandage roll and twisted with a stick. If used, it should be released every few minutes for a few seconds.

Gunshot

If your dog is accidentally shot with a shotgun, the damage that results is relative; it will depend on the distance from which he was shot, the type of load, the gauge of the shotgun, and what part of his body the pellets struck. If he was many yards away and took a few pellets in his rump, it isn't likely that the damage will be great. If he was close to the gun and some of the pellets struck him in the face, chest, or abdomen, an emergency may exist. There is nothing you can do in the field except to keep him warm and quiet; waste no time in getting Chip to a veterinarian.

Snake Bite

If Chip is bitten by a rattlesnake or other poisonous snake, the best first-aid is a fast car and minimal traffic. Pick up the dog immediately. Keep him very quiet. Carry him to the car and get him to your veterinarian as quickly as possible. Snake venom enters the blood stream and travels quickly in an active animal. There will be some tissue damage at the site of the bite, but don't cut and mutilate the area. Likewise, do not use a tourniquet. Ice packs are sometimes used over the bite wound to slow the venom's travel but be careful that you don't freeze the tissue.

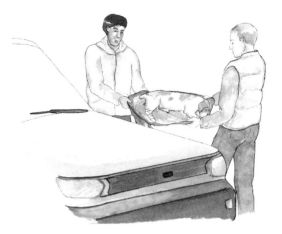

An emergency stretcher is used to transport the dog to the veterinarian.

Your veterinarian may dispense antivenin to you if rattlesnakes are common in your hunting area. The directions for its use will accompany the vials. Antivenin is expensive, has a short storage life, requires several doses for larger dogs, and is usually impractical to carry.

Puncture Wounds

The most common cause of a puncture is a sharp stick, and any deep puncture wound should receive immediate attention. When it involves the chest area, abdomen, or the upper

Minor pad injuries are protected with boots.

leg, leave the stick in place if feasible, pick up the dog, carry him to your car, and transport him to the veterinarian. If you attempt to remove the stick, you might cause hemorrhage or you may leave a piece of the stick lodged deep in the tissues. If the cause of the puncture is gone, apply pressure to the wound to control bleeding and get Chip to his veterinarian.

Foot Pad Lacerations

Lacerated pads are injuries that may be serious or minor, depending on their extent. Most hunting dogs manage to cut a pad at some time, and rarely are such wounds life threatening. If the pad laceration is extensive, stop the bleeding with a light pressure bandage and put Chip in his crate. If the laceration isn't extensive and hemorrhage control isn't a factor, it is OK to put boots (leather or plastic foot protectors) on him and continue hunting if Chip is comfortable and willing.

Immunization and Preventive Medicine

The breeder usually begins immunizations soon after puppies are weaned. These immunizations should be continued throughout the dog's life. The particular vaccination schedule for Chip should be designed for him and his lifestyle. The following discussion relates to contagious, infectious diseases that may be prevented by vaccinations at the appropriate time.

Canine Distemper

In spite of today's effective vaccines, canine distemper (CD) (Dog Plague or Hard Pad) is still a significant threat to young puppies. Its mortality rate, lack of a reliable cure, and easy transmission make it an important canine disease. Canine distemper is caused by a virus that attacks the dog's respiratory tract, intestinal tract, and brain. It often results in convulsions and death. The reservoir of infection for CD often exists in stray dog populations and wild carnivores such as raccoons, foxes, and minks.

When young unvaccinated pups contract CD, they may die suddenly with-

A stuffed pheasant is being used to train this pup to point.

out displaying any symptoms. More often, signs of infection include fever, loss of appetite, lethargy, dehydration, diarrhea, and vomiting. A yellow or green ocular discharge often accompanies infection, and coughing is another common sign of the disease. Some dogs may seem to respond to various treatments, only to succumb to convulsions and paralysis at a later date. Hardened pads, tooth enamel deficiencies, and permanent neurological signs such as blindness or twitching of extremities often affect those dogs that miraculously survive the disease.

There is no excuse for failure to vaccinate your puppy against this disease. The first of a series of CD vaccinations is given at about six weeks of age, and the vaccine is usually combined with other vaccines. Annual boosters are required. Be sure to keep Chip confined and away from any possible exposure until he has had at least his first two vaccinations.

Hepatitis

Infectious canine hepatitis is another contagious, incurable, fatal disease of dogs. It is highly communicable among dogs, but is not contagious to humans. Now known by the initials CAV-1 (canine adenovirus, type 1), it is a systemic disease that causes severe liver damage. Symptoms often mimic those of distemper, and it may cause sudden death in young pups.

Vaccines are highly effective in preventing CAV-1 and are usually combined with other immunizing agents. A series of vaccinations is begun at or shortly after 6 weeks of age, with annual boosters required.

Leptospirosis

Lepto is a devastating kidney disease that is sometimes fatal and is caused by a spirochete organism. This highly contagious infection is transmitted by urine from affected animals. It is more prevalent in male dogs than in females. The disease is also contagious to humans.

The signs of a lepto infection include lethargy, lack of appetite, thirst, rusty-colored urine, diarrhea, and vomiting. Affected dogs sometimes walk with a peculiar stilted, roach-backed gait. Treatment of a lepto infection may be successful, but permanent kidney damage that results from an infection can be serious. Leptospirosis vaccine is usually combined with CD and CAV-1 immunizing products.

Parvovirus and Coronavirus

Parvovirus and Coronavirus are among the more recently documented contagious, and sometimes fatal, canine diseases. Coronavirus infections are less often fatal than parvovirus. These viral diseases cause severe diarrhea, vomiting, dehydration, and depression, and they are especially devastating to puppies. They are spread from infected dogs by saliva, feces, vomit, or one-on-one contact. Humans are not susceptible to these viruses, but they may transmit the viruses on their shoes or clothes.

Supportive therapy sometimes improves the prognosis, but in young animals, sudden death is common. If vomiting and diarrhea are treated and dehydration is successfully controlled with intravenous fluid therapy, the dog may have a chance.

Vaccinations are usually given at or shortly after 6 weeks of age, with annual boosters also required. Consult with your veterinary practitioner about the use of those products.

Kennel Cough

A pair of respiratory diseases, caused by parainfluenza virus and *Bordetella* bacteria, cause coughing, fever, loss of appetite, and depression. They are highly contagious and are easily spread by aerosol (airborne

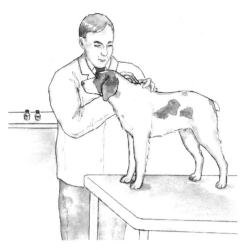

Dogs need to be vaccinated for a multitude of diseases.

droplets of saliva that are suspended in an affected dog's cough or sneeze). The areas commonly affected are the bronchial tubes, trachea, and throat.

Usually, uncomplicated kennel cough will pass in a week or two if the dog is rested and if the concurrent bacterial infections are treated. Kennel cough typically has a lower fatality rate than some of the diseases that were previously discussed, but it deserves serious consideration in your vaccination program.

Respiratory vaccines include intranasal types that are often less predictable than injectables, but their reliability is improving. Because of recent advances in vaccine research, consult with your local veterinarian about what product is best for your dog.

Lyme Disease

This is a relatively new disease of dogs. The deer tick is the carrier of this disease. In the past, Lyme disease has been more common in the northeastern and midwestern areas of the United States, but it continues to spread and is presently reported in 40 states. White-tailed deer and field mice are the principal hosts for the deer tick.

Lyme disease often causes lameness in the dog and is accompanied by heat, pain, and swelling of one or more joints. Body temperature is usually elevated, and affected dogs are listless. Early treatment is vital to the dog's recovery.

The risk of Lyme disease is related to the length of time that a tick is attached to your dog. When you find a tick on Chip take it off immediately. (See the discussion about ticks that follows for more information.) If you are in an area where deer ticks are commonly found, check your dog at least daily for their presence. They are tiny [about 0.1 inch diameter (.04 cm)], black or red and black, and they often look like a little dark mole on the skin. As they suck blood, they grow much larger, grayer, and a female tick sometimes reaches the size of a grape.

A Lyme disease vaccine is available but its efficacy is questionable,. Check with your veterinarian. Newer vaccines against Lyme disease are being produced, but are not generally available at this time. A reliable tick prevention program is another practical way to try to prevent this disease.

Rabies

This is a fatal disease of all warm-blooded animals. It is spread only by contact with the saliva of an infected animal; hence it usually follows bite wounds. The signs of rabies reflect brain changes. The average time lapse between an infected bite and signs of the disease (incubation period) is usually only two or three weeks but occasionally is several months. The rabies virus travels from the site of the bite to the brain via nerves. If the infecting bite occurs

on a foot, it results in a longer incubation period.

After reaching the brain, the rabies virus migrates to the salivary glands where it reproduces. The signs of rabies in a dog are varied. Sometimes the affected dog becomes aggressive and highly irritable. As the disease progresses, the dog may become paralyzed (dumb rabies) or vicious (furious rabies).

Vaccine for this important disease is usually administered later than other diseases. Many cities and counties have ordinances or laws that require rabies vaccinations to be administered when dogs reach three months of age, by or under the direction of, licensed and USDA accredited veterinarians. Those laws were made to address the public health significance of the disease.

Reservoirs of the rabies virus include carnivores such as skunks, raccoons, coyotes, bats, and other wildlife. Because this incurable and fatal disease can be transmitted to humans and all other warm-blooded animals, great emphasis is placed on rabies preventive programs.

Other Common Diseases

Gastric Torsion, Dilatation, and Bloat

This condition is more commonly seen in breeds that are larger than the Brittany but it can affect any dog. There are many theories regarding the cause of this often fatal condition. One possible factor is the practice of feeding a single heavy meal, then water, followed by exercise. Another is the practice of feeding the dog on the floor or ground, followed by activity. This seems to be an important factor in giant breeds.

In any event, about two to six hours after a meal, an affected dog suddenly begins to display abdominal bloat. Its stomach becomes distended; it repeatedly attempts to vomit, but is unable to do so, producing only thick saliva in small amounts. The veterinarian may attempt to pass a stomach tube to relieve the stomach gas, but those efforts are often futile.

The dog quickly becomes toxic, staggers, and experiences intense abdominal pain. Immediate surgery may save the pet, and corrective techniques are available to help prevent the condition from repeating itself. Unfortunately, by the time the dog reaches a veterinary hospital, he may be suffering from advanced toxemia and efforts to save him may be too late.

There are several measures to prevent this condition. Feed your dog when activity is at a minimum. Elevate the dog's food bowl to minimize air swallowing. Encourage frequent, small meals (free-choice feeding). When you feed the major meal of the day make sure that your Brittany is quiet thereafter. Don't allow the dog to engorge with water following a meal. Above all, curtail the activity of Chip after any meal.

Grass Awns

Whether your pet enjoys the freedom of a fenced yard, is confined to a dog run, or is a hunting companion, he is bound to encounter the nuisance of cheat grass or wild oats awns. The seeds of those plants are attached to little beards that catch in your socks when you walk though the grass. Those same little bearded awns can make their way into Chip's ears, causing great discomfort and necessitating a trip to your veterinarian for removal.

Grass awns also may catch in the hair between Chip's toes. If not discovered and removed promptly, the sharply pointed little seeds penetrate the skin and begin to migrate into the tissue, requiring minor surgery for removal.

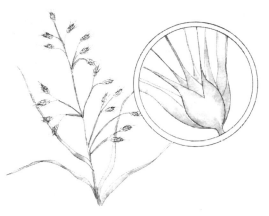

This sharp little awn can cause trouble in the ears or between the toes.

Intestinal Parasites

Intestinal parasites, especially tapeworms, roundworms, whipworms, hookworms, and coccidia may seriously affect the general health and vitality of puppies.

Roundworm larvae may remain hidden in cysts in females' tissues throughout their lives. During pregnancy, larvae migrate from those cysts into the fetuses and develop in the puppies' intestines where they mature and produce eggs. Roundworm eggs in a dog's feces are the sources of infestation for other dogs (and possibly under certain rare circumstances, for children). These eggs are identified on microscopic examination of feces.

A stool sample from your Brittany should be taken to your veterinarian at least once a year. If parasite ova (eggs) are found in the stool sample, your veterinarian will prescribe an appropriate medication.

Tapeworms are intestinal parasites that have secondary hosts. They aren't transmitted from dog to dog like other parasites. Tapeworms use deer, ground birds, rodents, or fleas as their secondary host. To become infested, the dog must consume part of one of these hosts. Fleas are probably the most common secondary host of tapeworms, and eating an infected flea can transmit the tapeworm to dogs.

Tapeworms aren't usually diagnosed by a stool sample because the tapeworm head remains attached to the lining of the dog's intestine. The body of the worm is composed of tiny segments, and it grows to enormous lengths. As it grows, the segments break off and pass out in the stool. Finding these small, white segments that look like tiny grains of rice, which are often stuck to the hair around the dog's anus diagnoses a tapeworm infestation.

Remember that worm medications are types of poisons. Be meticulous in calculating dosages and carefully administer the medication according to label directions. There is no single universal worm medication, and an especially perilous procedure is to "worm" all puppies, whether or not a parasite infestation has been diagnosed.

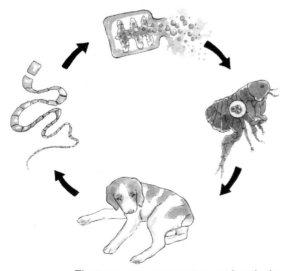

The tapeworm can grow to great lengths in the intestine, where it robs dogs of nutrition.

Heartworms

Microscopic heartworm larvae are transmitted from an infected dog by mosquitoes. The larvae develop inside the mosquito for a couple of weeks and are then injected into another dog when the mosquito bites it. After further maturing, the adult heartworms (that have reached up to a foot in length and are the diameter of a piece of twine), are found living in the dog's heart. If only a few are present, there may be no immediate outward signs, but if many are present, the animal can show dynamic symptoms of heart failure. In either case, an infected dog acts as a reservoir of infection for other dogs.

Heartworm was originally found in warm, humid areas of the country where mosquitoes prevailed, but in recent years, the disease has spread to nearly every part of the United States, including Alaska. Before a preventive program can be initiated, a blood test must show that there are no larvae circulating in your dog's blood stream. Heartworm prevention is accomplished by means of regular oral medication.

Skin Parasites

Dermatological problems such as fungus (ringworm) and mite infestations (mange) are often seen in weanling puppies. The most common mange mites are *Cheyletiella*, *Demodex*, *Psoroptes*, and *Sarcoptes*. Another mite, *Otodectes*, may parasitize ear canals of both cats and dogs.

As with other diseases, a definitive diagnosis must be made before treatment is initiated. Skin scrapings examined under a microscope will identify the mites responsible for mange lesions. Examination of earwax will identify ear mites. Skin scrapings, ultraviolet light, or cultures are used to identify fungal infections.

Lice are seen occasionally in some areas of the country and may be of the sucking or biting varieties. They are easily diagnosed and treated, because all life stages of the louse live on the dog. Topical treatment such as dips or medicated baths are usually satisfactory.

Don't rely on a universal mange dip or ringworm salve to cure skin diseases. Those products may create new problems while doing nothing to solve the original one.

Fleas

This pesky parasite is common in backyard or kenneled dogs, and heavy infestations are seen in warmer climates. The flea lives part of its life cycle off the dog and is therefore more difficult to treat successfully than lice. Fleas act as secondary hosts for tapeworms, and fleas' saliva often causes an allergic dermatitis on the dog that is confusing to diagnose and difficult to treat.

Fleas are illusive. They bite to make a small wound, from which they lap up the blood that oozes from the skin wound. Adult fleas have the ability to leap great distances; they sometimes land on a human, and they aren't terribly particular from whom they receive their meal. When a dog has fleas they will usually be found over his pelvic area or under his forelegs. One way to locate fleas is to run a fine-toothed comb carefully through the coat over the pelvis. The parasites will be caught between the flea comb's teeth, or they will jump from the hair in front of the comb. If the adult fleas aren't found, you may see some of their excreta (feces), appearing as tiny, black, comma-shaped debris.

Fleas are terribly irritating to a dog. They often stimulate licking, chewing, and scratching, and contribute to the formation of "hot spots," another serious skin condition.

If you suspect a flea problem, remember that this parasite is a part-

I'm really a hunting dog, but I love my creature comfort.

time resident of the dog. Once it arrives on its host, it feeds, mates, and lays eggs. The eggs are deposited on the dog and fall off in the doghouse, on your carpet, or wherever the pet happens to be. The eggs hatch into larvae that feed on dandruff and other organic debris in their environment. They pupate and emerge to begin looking for a host. The adult flea can live for more than 100 days without a blood meal.

If fleas are diagnosed, be sure to follow a long-term treatment program that uses products that are proven safe for the age of your Brittany.

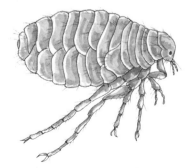
Fleas cause irritation when they bite, and they may transmit tapeworms.

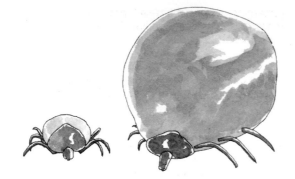

Ticks are loathsome creatures that transmit several serious dog diseases.

Several new flea repellent products are available from your veterinarian. Some are in tablet form and are given orally, whereas others are in liquid form and are applied topically on the skin once a month. Some kill the flea eggs; others only kill the adult. Ask your veterinarian about the products and their safety, cost, and effectiveness.

New biological control programs have been initiated in some areas. One involves the yard application of tiny nematodes (worms) that consume flea eggs but are harmless to humans and pets. Others involve the use of insect growth regulators that interfere with the flea's life cycle.

A new generation of flea collars are also available to repel the parasites rather than killing them after they have bitten the dog.

Organic products such as pyrethrum and other "natural" insecticides are usually thought of as "safer." That may or may not be the case, but they are much less effective than the contemporary products. An electronic collar is available that emits high-frequency sounds that are supposed to repel fleas, but its effectiveness is suspect.

Do not use oral medication, dips, sprays, powders, medicated collars, or other drugs that are not labeled for the specific age and weight of your Brittany. Beware of all systemic medications in a pregnant or lactating female.

Ticks

Adult ticks bury their heads in a dog's skin and suck blood for days at a time. The males are about the size of a pinhead; females often reach the size of a grape when they fill with blood. After a blood meal, ticks fall off, lay thousands of eggs and die. Their other life stages may be completed on the dog (as in the brown dog tick), or they may use birds, deer, rodents, or other mammals for secondary hosts.

If you find a tick on Chip, grasp it as close to his skin as possible with a pair of tweezers or forceps. With firm, steady traction, pull it out. Ticks are often found under the collar, under the forelegs, around the ears, and over the withers.

Don't panic if the tick's head breaks off. Contrary to popular belief, the imbedded part of the tick that remains in the dog shouldn't cause a problem. After you have extracted the tick, destroy it by placing it in alcohol. Don't try to drown a tick in water, don't squash it, and don't handle the tick with bare fingers.

Where the tick was embedded clean the skin with alcohol or another disinfectant once or twice daily for several days. This will keep the scab off and allow drainage from the wound that the tick left.

A common belief is that ticks will be forced to detach if you heat their bodies with the flame of a match or the hot tip of a soldering iron. Heat really doesn't hasten their exit, and a flame may be hazardous to your dog. It is also occasionally advised that if a drop of acetone, alcohol, or nail-polish remover is placed on the tick, it will release its hold quickly. The theory is that the rapid evaporation of such products cool the tick and causes it to release its hold. That idea has more credibility than heating the tick, but it doesn't work every time. (Please don't combine heat and cooling. If you apply a combustible fluid, then light a match your dog might go up in flames.)

Tickborne Diseases

Lyme disease was discussed under diseases that may be prevented by vaccine.

Ehrlichiosis is another tickborne disease. It is transmitted by the brown dog tick and is a serious disease, manifested by nosebleeds, swelling of the limbs, anemia, and many other signs. It can be fatal if not treated early and adequately.

Hereditary Conditions

Monorchidism

Male dogs are born with both testicles positioned in their abdomen. Soon after birth, or by 30 or 40 days of age, the testicles should be descended into the scrotum. Testicular retention is hereditary, but the genetic mechanism is poorly understood.

Monorchidism is a condition in which one testicle is retained and the other is normally descended. Monorchid males are able to breed and are fertile. Such dogs should be neutered at or soon after puberty; retained testicles often develop malignant tumors. Due to the hereditability of this condition, monorchid males should never be used for breeding. An occasional Brittany is seen with monorchidism.

Cryptorchidism

Cryptorchids are males with both testicles retained in the abdomen. They are typically sterile but not impotent. They will mount and breed females, but usually can't produce offspring. Cryptorchid dogs should be neutered at or shortly after reaching puberty to prevent the development of malignant tumors later in life. Cryptorchids are rare in the Brittany.

Epilepsy

This convulsive disorder is thought to be inherited. It may be triggered by injury, tumors, or possibly certain infections, but for the most part, it must be considered genetic in origin. Fortunately, it is treatable. Unfortunately, the condition doesn't show up until the affected dog is several years old, so it is difficult to breed out of a strain or bloodline. Epilepsy is reported fairly commonly in Brittanys, and those animals shouldn't be used in a breeding program.

Canine Hip Dysplasia

This controversial disease causes hind leg lameness that sometimes doesn't appear until the dog is an adult. Canine hip dysplasia (CHD), or a predisposition to it, is undoubtedly hereditary, but in a complex way. It is prevalent to some degree in all large

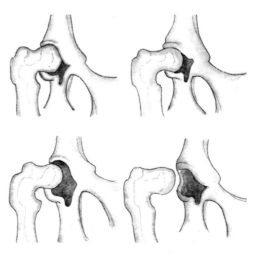

Hip dysplasia is a complex, hereditary disease.

A fine Brittany in excellent health.

and in many small purebred dogs. Dogs who have their hips x-rayed and have those x-rays checked by the Orthopedic Foundation for Animals (OFA) and are certified clear of the disease may (but rarely) produce affected puppies. In fact, CHD may appear in dogs from bloodlines that are certified "clear" for several generations.

Canine hip dysplasia involves the head (ball) of the femur and the acetabulum (pelvic hip socket). As the disease develops, the acetabulum and femoral head are often malformed and don't fit together as they should. In time, arthritis usually results from the condition, causing pain, inflammation, and lameness.

Canine hip dysplasia is a relative condition, and all dogs aren't equally affected. The degree of lameness depends on the amount of displacement of the femoral head and the degree of damage to the joint cartilage that has been caused by the deformity. Signs of the disease usually appear clinically by two or three years of age, but occasionally they are delayed six or seven years. Signs of CHD may appear in one hind leg (unilateral) or both hind legs (bilateral), causing difficulty in getting up from a lying or sitting position and lameness when walking. It may progress to a level wherein the dog can't get up or walk. Those dogs are usually thin and are in pain most of the time.

Treatments include hip replacement, other surgical techniques to relieve pain, anti-inflammatory drugs, and acupuncture. None of the treatments or medication will cure the disease and only the prudent selection of breeding stock can prevent the condition from occurring. X-rays of dogs younger than two years of age are not conclusive.

The Brittany has an incidence of CHD, but it is probably no greater than many other hunting breeds.

The OFA address is found in the back of this book.

Progressive Retinal Atrophy

Progressive retinal atrophy (PRA) is a serious hereditary eye condition that is seen clinically by five years of age. It is caused by degeneration of cells that are located in the retinas of the eyes, and the disease leaves the dog unable to see stationary objects.

Examination of breeding stock for this disease is critically important. (See CERF in the back of this book.) A few affected dogs are treated, but a cure is unlikely. A dog affected with PRA may lose its vision, but blindness isn't fatal. If the vision diminishes slowly, the dog will adapt and live a normal life span as a pet. Progressive retinal atrophy is occasionally reported in Brittanys.

Other Hereditary Conditions

Several other hereditary diseases are reported to occur in the Brittany in *Medical and Genetic Aspects of Purebred Dogs.* They include hemophilia A (factor VIII or antihemophilic factor deficiency) which causes prolonged bleeding, luxating patellas, overbite, underbite, and lip fold dermatitis.

Brittany breeders have reported the incidence of several other hereditary diseases. They include hypothyroidism, cardiomyopathy (heart failure), diabetes mellitus, diabetes insipidus, esophageal stenosis, and amyotrophic lateral sclerosis (Lou Gehrig's disease). The incidence of these conditions is probably very low.

Diseases of the Aging Brittany

Brood Bitch Diseases

If your Brittany has had no health problems and has raised puppies she should be retired by six or seven years of age. Earlier retirement is prudent if she has had breeding complications of any kind.

Although menopause does not occur in canines, reproductive lives of females ends much earlier than those of males. By about six years of age, a Brittany dam has usually passed her productive peak, although she continues to cycle and exhibit normal heat periods. Reproductive problems are likely to increase with each passing year, and the bitch's health is at risk.

The best advice for Brittany owners is to retire your companion before serious age-related maladies begin to show up. When the decision is made to retire her from reproductive or showing duties, schedule an ovariohysterectomy (spay). Spay operations in older females are somewhat more difficult to perform, and there are slightly higher risks involved than in young animals, but those risks are minor compared to the risks of pyometra, tumors, and mammary cancer. *Ovariohysterectomy is the best insurance policy you can buy for your retired female Brittany.*

Metritis and Pyometra (Uterine Infection)

These diseases frequently affect unspayed bitches. Dystocias (difficult births), combined with prolonged labor seem to increase the probability of uterine infections. This infectious disease is sometimes fatal in young and middle-aged females, but its danger is multiplied many times in older animals. It can be averted by ovariohysterectomy.

Pyometra is an extremely dangerous type of uterine infection that occurs most commonly in aged unspayed females.

Mammary Tumors

Breast tumors account for nearly half of all canine tumor cases and at least half of these are malignant. They may occur at any age, but are more common in females older than six years old. If your dog is spayed at or before puberty, the risk of mammary tumors is negligible. However, each time the female comes in heat her predisposition for mammary tumors increases.

Euthanasia

Putting a dog to sleep (euthanasia) is a subject we all hate to discuss. It would be so convenient if our old dogs wouldn't suffer from their infirmities, and when their time is up, they would lay down and die.

Unfortunately, it doesn't often happen that way and that's the reason for euthanasia. It is the final act of kindness and of stewardship that we can perform for our companions. When the lethal product is administered properly, a dog suffers no fear or apprehension. Your veterinarian will give your old pet an injection into a vein, and his life will be over in a few seconds. You can stay with Chip to the last or go to another room—that's up to you. If you are going to cry and fall apart at the seams, it's probably easier on the dog if you stay away. If you can hold him, giving him calm assurance, it's better if you are there. In any case, euthanasia, in competent hands, may be better than watching your pet die slowly from an incurable illness.

Brittany Breeding

Few people buy their first Brittany with the idea of breeding her and raising puppies. Many established breeders started out with a pet or companion dog, only to be fascinated by the breed at a later date. What they have discovered is that Brittany breeding offers a world of memorable experiences; it is a fulfilling hobby. The joy of watching Jill win titles and ribbons is a thrill that is surpassed only by raising a truly fine litter of Brittany puppies. Unfortunately, there are many downsides to that story that must be mentioned.

Breeding to Improve the Brittany

Brittanys are relatively popular dogs at this time, and their popularity encourages many amateur breeders to enter the scene, looking for a fast buck. These amateur breeders denigrate the breed and fill the market with average and below average dogs; don't join their ranks! Is your primary reason for breeding Jill to improve the breed by producing excellent quality show or field dogs? Will you strive to raise puppies that have predictable, trustworthy temperaments, or is your motive primarily monetary? You might be surprised to learn how little money is made from dog breeding.

Breeding high-quality dogs, especially dual-purpose dogs, is expensive. The only legitimate reason for breeding your Brittany is to improve the breed. If you can't do that, better give it up. A good stud dog demands—and is worth—a high stud fee. Only the best females should be bred to the very best males. To do any less isn't fair to the beautiful Brittany.

Breeding plans break down when greedy amateurs engage in backyard breeding programs, often doing the breed more harm than good. Too many times a cute seven-month-old female is bred to a neighbor's nice little one-year-old male, with disastrous results. If both parents are AKC registered, the pups are all eligible for registration, regardless of their quality. They are offered to the public as AKC registered Brittanys, and every fault and hereditary deformity imaginable may be propagated.

You can't raise show-quality pups from a pet-quality dam or sire. If the dam hasn't proved herself in shows, trials, or under the gun, the chances are good that her puppies will not do any better. It isn't likely that you will raise pups with great temperaments from a bitch or sire that is difficult to handle. Hopefully, before entering into a breeding program, you will consider those sobering thoughts.

If you decide to produce a litter from Jill, formulate a plan in advance for the probable markets for her pups. There are several pet-quality pups in every litter. Be certain that you can place all the pups in good homes before you progress any further. Find out how many Brittany puppies are presently offered for sale in your area. If there is an abundance, it might be better to wait six months.

Considerations Before Breeding

Although veterinary examinations of the prospective parents will reveal major hereditary faults, it is recommended that you go a step further before you embark on a career in

It is expensive to breed quality Brittanys.

breed. If Jill is primarily a hunter, ask the advice of trainers and handlers that are experienced with field trials or gun dogs. Slight discrepancies from the breed standard are expected, since there is no such thing as a perfect Brittany. However, if both sire and dam display the same minor imperfections, their progeny may exhibit major faults.

Jill and the chosen sire should be physically examined by a veterinarian (preferably the same one) who has been furnished with the breeding and health histories of both animals. The healthcare professional will want to examine for, or see certifications of, normal hip conformation for both the male and female. Keep in mind that OFA hip certification isn't done until the dogs are more than two years old. Congenital eye diseases and other hereditary problems should also be considered.

A maiden bitch should ideally be bred to a stud who has produced excellent pups from previous matings. Hopefully he will have sired pups from a bitch that is related to Jill. The quality of his progeny is one measure of his value. His conformation, temperament, and ability should be exemplary.

Brittany breeding. Every bitch has a few shortcomings that may influence the selection of a stud. Ask a successful Brittany breeder to fault Jill. If primarily interested in conformation shows, this might be someone with experience in judging or showing the

Pedigree Examination

Genetic considerations must be studied before Jill is bred. Her background should be compatible with the sire's background. If they are distantly related that should present no problem, but inbreeding and line breeding should be left to the experts. As a novice breeder, you should enlist the aid of an experienced breeder. Study the pedigrees of both sire and dam carefully. Look at pictures and the accomplishments of the dogs that are listed. Don't fall into the many traps that ensnare beginners, such as the notion that if a dog wins its championship it is bound to produce champions.

Sometimes the best pups are kept a few weeks after weaning.

It will take many phone calls to place this litter of eight.

If you bought Jill as the most promising pup of a good litter and she has lived up to expectations, she may be a good brood bitch. If you breed her to a proven male with a similar background, one that has produced excellent puppies from a bitch with a pedigree that is similar to your bitch's, you might be on a roll.

The Responsibility of an Ethical Breeder

Before you think of breeding Jill, think of the six to eight puppies that will result from the breeding. If you are active in either a breed club or a hunting club, you're not likely to encounter any problem finding good homes for most of your pups. Those pups that remain after the best prospects are gone are equally entitled to good homes. If you planned well, the pet-quality pups should be placed into companion-dog homes or with week-end shooters. Advertising in newsletters will usually locate additional placements, but you should always interview prospective buyers before you release a pup to a new home.

Be sure the buyers know what they are getting. If the pup isn't outstanding, make the buyers aware that the pup is not a breeding or showing prospect. Likewise, you may want to consider withholding registration, limited registration, or co-ownership of the pet-quality pup until proof of neutering is produced. Another approach that has worked is to put an enormous price on the puppy and then refund a fair share of that price to the new owners after the pup has been neutered. Don't contribute to the efforts and income of unethical breeders, and don't be a careless Brittany breeder.

A complete discussion of canine reproduction is discussed in *The Complete Book of Dog Breeding* (Rice, 1996, *Barron's Educational Series.*)

Spaying or Neutering

If you decide against raising puppies, spaying or neutering your Brittany is an excellent idea. The term "spay" means to render a female incapable of producing puppies by removing her internal reproductive organs. A small incision is made on the midline of her abdomen, and her uterus and both ovaries are surgically removed. She is hospitalized for this procedure, which requires general anesthesia.

This operation is permanent and can't be reversed. Once it is done, her estrus cycles will cease. There is virtually no danger of her developing mammary tumors (breast cancer) if she is spayed before her first season. There is practically no danger to Jill's life under normal circumstances. Surgical risks increase with age, obesity, or illness.

Spaying a young female has no appreciable negative side effects. Jill won't gain weight because she is spayed nor will she become lazy. She will be as good a bird dog as if she were intact. She may even be a better hunting dog because she will never come into heat during bird season.

Neutering of a male means to surgically remove both testicles. There are few, if any, side effects to this operation. Neutering Chip may make him more docile or less aggressive, although that is not always true. He is not likely to gain weight unless he is overfed or under exercised nor will he become lethargic. He, like Jill, will still be as active as he would have been if left intact.

Neutering of a male removes his sexual desire and is not the same as a vasectomy. A vasectomy involves surgically rendering a male incapable of producing puppies, but does not change the hormonal levels that stimulate sexual desire.

Registering and Showing Your Brittany

The American Kennel Club

The AKC has registered at least one million dogs each year since 1970. In 1996, 1,332,557 purebred dogs were registered. It is the largest and probably the oldest U.S. kennel club. Founded in 1884, the AKC is a nonprofit organization dedicated to the welfare and advancement of purebred dogs.

The AKC does not license kennels or individual dog breeders, but does train and license dog show judges. It adopts and enforces rules and regulations governing dog shows and other purebred canine exhibitions. The events that are held under AKC rules include conformation dog shows, obedience trials, agility contests, tracking trials, field trials, hunting tests, and herding tests and trials.

The registry maintains the standards of all breeds recognized by the club. AKC registers 143 breeds that are separated into seven groups for the purpose of exhibition. The Brittany is included in the Sporting group; the other six groups are Hound, Working, Terrier, Toy, Non-sporting, and Herding. Perhaps this organization's greatest contribution is the information they provide to anyone who is interested in promoting dog ownership and stewardship. Although there are other U.S. dog registries, the AKC is the most influential.

Litter Registration

Data for the following discussion was taken from various AKC documents. The policies and rules of other registries may vary, but the principles are the same.

When a litter is born, the owners of both sire and dam complete and sign a Litter Registration Application form that is sent to the registry, accompanied by an appropriate fee. When the application is received, AKC mails a "litter kit" to the dam's owner. It includes a blue-colored, partially completed registration application form for each puppy. One of those blue slips should accompany each puppy when it is sold.

The blue form lists the AKC litter registration number, the sire and dam's registration numbers, breeder information, and the sex of the pup. The breeder completes the form to show the puppy's color and markings, date purchased, and the buyer's name and address.

The puppy may also be named on the blue slip, but be forewarned that once a dog's name is registered it can't be changed. AKC invites complex names to better identify each dog. Simple names like Chip or Jill just won't do! This form should be signed by the buyer and sent to the AKC with a fee.

After the blue slip is completed and mailed to the registry with a fee, a permanent *AKC Registration Certificate* is printed and mailed to the new owner. Co-ownership or limited registration of purebred dogs is also possible.

Pedigrees

A pedigree is a genealogical document—a family tree. It is of great

Brittanys are great show dogs.

value, almost indispensable, if the dog is bred. It may contain three or four generations of a registered dog's ancestry. Breeders often prepare pedigrees on blank forms or on computer formats. Although these are not official documents, if accurate, they furnish the same information as an AKC pedigree.

If an official AKC pedigree is desired, it can be purchased from the registry for a fee. These documents list AKC exhibition titles as well as the names and registration numbers of three or four generations of the dog's ancestors. An indication of the dog's hip conformation as determined by the OFA may be included, and the coat colors of your dog's ancestors can be shown on the pedigree as well.

Conformation Shows

Those dog owners whose interests lie in other directions sometimes call conformation competition (dog shows) "beauty pageants." That term isn't really fair and doesn't quite cover the subject. Conformation shows are designed to promote registered pure-bred dogs and to identify breeding stock or potential breeding stock. In order to be eligible for showing, a dog must be intact, that is not spayed or neutered. It must be free of hereditary diseases and deformities to the best of the judges' knowledge. In order to win in a show, the exhibited dog must be of the correct size and marked correctly. It must have the correct type and amount of coat and move with a sound and balanced gait.

The ideal Brittany is one that matches the breed standard that is written by Brittany clubs and adopted by the AKC. Dog shows are designed to judge dogs of the same breed and sex against one another, and points are awarded for specific class wins, depending on the number of competitors entered.

A Champion being awarded her due.

This is how a Brittany is "stacked."

Titles

A number of titles are assigned to winners of competitive events that are sanctioned by the AKC. The AKC currently regulates and furnishes judges for seven events. Of those, Brittanys may compete in five (they have been covered in a previous chapter). The methods of assigning the points and wins required to receive titles in those disciplines are briefly discussed in the chapter on work for your Brittany on pages 60–70. The remaining event for which registered Brittanys are eligible is conformation showing. That endeavor is treated separately here because it represents a different but important phase of Brittany ownership.

Although having a dog that wins a prestigious title is a rewarding experience for the Brittany owner, a feeling of accomplishment will come with each near miss as well. Each time Chip competes, you learn something of the Brittany, and he learns from you. To own a dog that glides across the ring and receives the applause of the bystanders gives you a feeling of pride. To show well is an accomplishment for the dog and for the handler. To win is ecstasy!

The title awarded to an animal that has proved its merit by earning sufficient points according to AKC rules is "Champion of Record." That title is abbreviated "Ch." and is added as a prefix to a dog's AKC registered name. A Champion of Record is a dog that has accumulated at least 15 points that have been awarded by at least three different judges. The points awarded vary according to the number of dogs of the same breed that are entered and cannot exceed five at any show. Only two dogs at each show earn points. The total points leading to championship must include two wins of no less than three points each (major wins). To earn a Champion of Record Title is not as easy as it may seem!

Show Dogs

All registered Brittanys can be entered in a show, provided that they have reached the minimal age of six months, are physically normal, and have been trained sufficiently to behave in the ring.

A dog must be well trained and happy to place well in dog shows.

Show dogs must be clean and groomed, but Brittanys require practically no special coat trimming to be shown. Their coats may be trimmed on the neck and shoulders to avoid appearing unkempt. The hair must be thinned never clipped. Sometimes excessive foot hair is a problem, and it may also be thinned. Nails, of course, should be trimmed.

Show dogs must be manageable and trustworthy, because control is a vital part of participation in shows. The Brittany breed standard includes temperament qualities that are also judged. It states that the dog should be a happy, alert dog—neither mean nor shy.

Competing dogs are not allowed in the conformation show ring if they have any of the disqualifications that are listed in the standard. In the Brittany, that includes a size disqualification for dogs that are under 17½ inches (44.5 cm) tall, or more than 20½ inches (52 cm) tall. A Brittany's nose pad or rubber must be pigmented fawn, tan, brown, or pink, and a black nose is a disqualification. Another disqualification for Brittanys is any black color in its coat. A dog with those disqualifications is barred from future conformation show exhibition.

Before making a decision to begin a show career for your pup, consult with Brittany breeders in your local club. Have Chip "faulted" or judged by someone who has been involved with the breed for a while and has shown dogs. If the pup isn't mature enough or has an obvious problem, the experienced person should be able to point it out to you.

If it appears that Chip has the quality to win, enroll him in classes. Many specialty clubs and all-breed dog clubs have regular conformation classes for novice dogs. Enter Chip in fun matches for experience (yours and his). If all goes well in the classes and matches, you are ready for the big time. If you decide to enter him in a dog show, you may elect to exhibit him yourself or you can hire a professional handler.

A show dog and his handler must be trained. Chip must obey his handler instantly, and he must look to the handler for direction. He can't be easily distracted and must stand very still when the judge runs his hands over the dog. Chip can't resent being lifted a tiny bit by the tail or having his scrotum handled when the judge checks to ascertain that he has normal testicles. The judge will also open Chip's lips to expose his bite. The dog must accept these invasions of privacy with good nature, and a little tail wagging doesn't hurt his chances either.

Handlers

An owner or handler shouldn't try to exhibit a dog without the benefit of some classes and instruction. Breed clubs and all-breed clubs usually hold handler classes at least once a year. If a child hopes to handle the family dog in an AKC show, start the youngster's junior-handling education early. Although no preference is given to children handlers, a well-dressed child handling a fine Brittany will quickly get the attention of the audience and judge.

Prospective handlers should attend dog shows to see what is required. When the judge tells the handler *"Up and back,"* the reaction should be instantaneous. Sometimes judges call their top dogs out of competition very quietly, and the handler must listen carefully. Nothing is more embarrassing than having your dog chosen and not realizing it until the judge shouts *"Brittany,"* to the gallery's amusement.

Entries

The AKC is particular about entries. Everything must be in order on the dog's registration, and the application must be correctly filed and mailed by a deadline date. Your dog will compete against other Brittanys of the same sex.

Breed Standard

The Official Standard for the Brittany can be obtained from your Brittany club or from the AKC. Highlights from that standard are given here.

The Brittany is a dog that appears compact and agile, one that can cover ground easily. It displays the quick movements of an athlete. The Brittany weighs between 30 and 40 pounds (13.5 to 18 kg) and has a height that equals its length, measured from the point of the forechest to the rear of the rump.

The Brittany expression should be eager, alert, and it has soft amber-colored eyes that are well set in the head and protected by heavy eyebrows. The Brittany's ears should be set high, above the level of the eyes, and should be short, triangular, and rounded. The muzzle should be medium length. A dish face, snipy, or Roman nose is undesirable. A two-tone nose pad or lips with flews are undesirable, and the Brittany's bite is a true scissors, never overshot or undershot.

The neck should be of medium length and well set into sloping shoulders. The Brittany's topline slopes slightly from the shoulders to the root of the tail. A Brittany has a deep chest, well-sprung ribs, and a short, straight back that isn't swayed or roached. The loin is short and strong and not tucked up or flabby. The Brittany may be tailless or have a tail of less than 4 inches (10.16 cm) long that may be natural or docked.

A Brittany's shoulders are sloping and muscular with the shoulder blade and upper arm forming nearly a 90 degree angle. Its front legs are perpendicular, clean, and graceful. The elbows and feet turn neither inward

A local club competition.

nor outward, and the pasterns are slightly sloped. The Brittany's feet are smaller than spaniels with well-arched toes and thick pads.

The Brittany's hindquarters are broad, strong, and muscular with powerful thighs and well-bent stifles. The hocks must not be placed far out behind the dog, and the stifles must not be turned outward resulting in a cow hock. The rear pasterns are moderately short and point neither inward nor outward.

Brittanys have dense, flat, or wavy coats that are never curly. Coat texture is neither wiry nor silky. Some feathering is seen on the legs, but never in abundance. The Brittany skin should be fine and fairly loose, so as to roll with briar and sticks of the field, thus resisting tearing.

The Brittany colors are orange and white or liver and white in either clear or roan patterns, with some ticking preferable. Washed out colors are undesirable. Tri-colors consisting of liver, white, and orange are not disqualified, but neither are they desirable. Black markings constitute disqualification.

The Brittany is a clean-moving dog, one that covers ground well. At a trot, the Brittany's hind foot should step into or beyond the print left by the forefoot.

Judging

AKC judges mentally compare each dog in the class with the "perfect" Brittany as described by the standard. Allowances are made for age, maturity, and differences between the sexes. The judge must be conversant with virtually every point in the breed standard and make placements accordingly.

Conformation dogs are not judged on the basis of the breed standard alone. Judges have the responsibility to consider the dog's attitude and conditioning. Training and willingness are important parts of showing, and a dog that is enjoying itself has a better chance at winning than one that is just going through the motions.

Types of Shows

There are two types of dog shows: specialty and all-breed events. Specialty shows are limited to dogs of a particular breed or group of similar breeds. All-breed shows are unlimited, and all registered dogs may be entered. Individual dog clubs manage the shows that are held under AKC rules. Every recognized breed has a national parent club as well as a local specialty clubs.

The parent club has the responsibility of revising and clarifying the official standards of their breed, and after the parent club has approved changes, they can be submitted to the AKC for its final approval.

Classes

There are five classes in which a dog may compete for points toward its

In the show ring.

championship. The puppy class is often divided into two groups: six to nine months and nine to twelve months. The novice class, bred-by-exhibitor class, American-bred class, and open class are the others in which dogs may compete.

Judging of every breed follows the same routine, and the males compete only with other males, and bitches are judged against other bitches. The reason for which a dog was bred has no bearing on how it is judged in a conformation show.

First the puppy dogs (males) are judged, with four placements awarded to each class with the first place remaining in competition.

The Novice dogs, Bred-by-Exhibitor, American-bred, and Open dog classes (males) are judged individually and the first-place dogs from each class are brought back into the ring to compete again. This judging of first-place winners is called the Winners Class, and the winner of this class is called the Winners Dog. That dog receives

Every Brittany is a winner in the heart of its owner.

championship points at the show. The dog that placed second to the Winners Dog in its original class is brought into the ring to compete with the other class winners for Reserve Winners Dog. If the Winners Dog is disqualified by the AKC for any reason, the Reserve Winners Dog receives the points.

The process is then repeated for the bitches to find the Winners Bitch (the only bitch to receive points at the show) and Reserve Winners Bitch.

The next class to be judged is composed of all entered Champions of Record (male and female), the Winners Dog, and the Winners Bitch. This is called the Best of Breed class, and from it is selected the single animal

that the judge considers the Best of Breed in the show. Then the judge selects the Best of Winners from the Winners Dog and Winners Bitch. If one of those two dogs have already been selected as Best of Breed, that animal is automatically the Best of Winners. Finally, a Best of Opposite Sex is chosen from the class.

In a specialty show, that concludes the judging. In an all-breed show, the Best of Breed winner competes in its group for placement in the group. Dogs chosen as best in each of the seven groups competes for Best in Show.

In dual-purpose dogs (dogs that are trained for field as well as conformation showing), the ultimate title of dual champion is awarded to dogs that have earned their Champion of Record title in conformation shows, as well as a Field Champion title in field trials. It designates a dog of superior conformation in which few faults were found. It is a talented hunter that has been judged against other field dogs and hasn't come away wanting. A Triple Champion is a dog that has earned a Field Champion title, a Champion of Record title, and an Obedience Trial Champion title. This dog would be the ultimate in perfection to own. For the average Brittany owner however, perhaps that goal is a bit high; it requires thousands of hours of training and work to accomplish. AKC titles are only awarded to Chip after many flawless performances in field trials, conformation shows, or occasionally in obedience, agility, or tracking—but you and I know that in his heart and in the hearts of his owners, every Brittany is a champion!

Useful Literature and Addresses

Clubs

Amateur Field Trial Clubs of America
360 Winchester Lane
Stanton, TN 38069

American Brittany Club
2036 North 48th Avenue
Omaha, NE 68104

American Kennel Club
51 Madison Avenue
New York, NY 10010
For Registration, Records, Litter
    Information:
5580 Centerview Drive
Raleigh, NC 27606

Canadian Kennel Club
111 Eglington Avenue
Toronto 12, Ontario
Canada

Kennel Club, The
1-4 Clargis St
Picadilly
London W7Y8AB
England

National Shoot to Retrieve
    Association
226 North Mill St #2
Plainfield, IN 46168

North American Versatile Hunting
    Dog Association
Box 529
Arlington Heights, IL 60006

Periodicals

Dog World
29 North Wacker Drive
Chicago, IL 60606

AKC Gazette
51 Madison Avenue
New York, NY 10010

American Field, The
542 South Dearborn St.
Chicago, IL 60605

Organizations

Canine Eye Registry Foundation
    (CERF)
South Campus Court, Building C
West Lafayette, IN 47907

Institute for Genetic Disease Control
    (GDC)
P.O. Box 222
Davis, CA 95617

Owner Handler Association of
    America, Inc.
Mrs. Mildred Mash
6 Michaels Lane (c)
Old Brookville, NY 11545

Orthopedic Foundation for Animals
    (OFA)
2300 Nifong Blvd.
Columbia, MO 65201

Anxious for the hunt.

Books

Alderton, David. *Dogs,* New York: DK Publishing Company, 1993.

American Kennel Club. *The Complete Dog Book,* New York: Macmillan Publishing Co., 1992.

Carmel, Rheta. *The Book of The American Brittany,* Aledo TX: American Brittany Club, Inc., 1980.

Clark, Ross D. and Stainer, Joan R. *Medical & Genetic Aspects of Pure-bred Dogs,* Fairway, KS and St. Simons Island GA: Forum Publications, Inc., 1994.

Davis, Henry P. *Modern Dog Encyclopedia,* Harrisburg, Pennsylvania: The Stackpole Company, 1958.

Lorenz, Michael D. and Cornelius, Larry M. *Small Animal Medical Diagnosis*, 2nd ed. Philadelphia; J.B. Lippincott Company, 1993.

Rice, Dan F. *The Complete Book of Dog Breeding,* New York: Barron's Educational Series, 1997.

Riddle, Maxwell, *The New Complete Brittany,* New York: Howell Book House, 1987.

Yamazaki, Tetsu. *Legacy of the Dog,* San Francisco: Chronicle Books, 1995.

Just taking it easy in the backyard.

This old-timer is an agile hunter.

Index

One of Europe's oldest hunting breeds, the affable Brittany is an ideal companion dog for weekend hunting and field trial enthusiasts.